The Best Option Strategies:

A "Hands On" Guide to Making Money with Options

Volume 2

Iron Condors

Mark D Wolfinger

Options for Rookies Books

Iron Condors

Mark D Wolfinger

This is Book THREE in a series of educational and informative books for option traders.

Requests to the publisher should be addressed to Mark D Wolfinger; 1717 Dobson Street; Evanston, IL 60202

ASIN: B00M7A3HXI

The Purpose of this Series of Books

These e-books are designed to introduce the reader to one specific option strategy. This is Volume 2: Iron Condors. This book contains information for the novice as well as for the more experienced trader.

Each volume contains a thorough discussion of one, low-risk option strategy. There are no get rich quick schemes, nor promises of enormous profits. These books represent the 'nuts and bolts' of using options in strategies that work.

The efficient trader has more than one strategy in his/her arsenal of trade ideas and chooses an appropriate method that depends on current market conditions. Don't fall in love with one strategy, forsaking all others.

Volume 2 is for the reader who has a neutral market bias and wants to earn money from the passage of time. This strategy works best when the stock market trades within a range, and should be avoided when the market is in a steady unidirectional trend. Extremely volatile markets are difficult for the iron condor trader, but the experienced and *successful* trader should be able to handle most situations.

If you are encountering options for the first time, this book is not (yet) for you. Begin your basic options education with my classic primer: *The Rookie's Guide to Options, 2nd edition*, 2013.

This is VOLUME 2: **Iron Condors**

Volume 0: Introduction to Options: The Basics

Volume 1: Writing Naked Puts

Table of Contents

Introduction

Iron Condors is the third book in a series that offers a hands-on education for some of the most useful option strategies. It is intended to be quite different from all other books you may have read that discuss this versatile option strategy.

One popular idea is that iron condors can be used to generate a steady monthly income stream. Although there is truth to that idea, it is a vast oversimplification. Iron condors do provide an income stream for disciplined traders who understand (a) the importance of risk management and (b) how and when to trade iron condors.

If you have been led to believe that iron condors are a 'set it and forget it' strategy, I will try to get that idea out of your head. These positions require careful monitoring, and the frequency depends on the specific options that comprise the iron condor. It is never a position to initiate and then ignore.

Most iron condors – at least the type that I recommend as suitable for the majority of traders – require some active decision making as long as the position remains in your portfolio. Sometimes that decision requires action to reduce risk. At other times, the decision will be to do nothing and continue to hold. But make no mistake, deciding to hold is a real decision – not to be made lightly.

Another decision involves a pre-planned (I encourage the preparation of a trade plan for each trade) exit to lock in the profit. As the trade progresses, and when the position is working and profits accumulate, it becomes a daily decision: hold or exit. It is important to avoid being greedy; it is important to recognize when there is just too little remaining profit potential in the trade to warrant holding. That is where the trade plan, and the target profit, can help you become a disciplined trader.

Closing the position may be easy and pleasurable, such as when you earn the target profit before expiration arrives.

However, it could also be a gut-wrenching decision that locks in a loss and is made because it is essential to take some risk-reducing action for a position that has not worked as planned.

Expect to learn the basic concepts of trading iron condors:

--How to decide which options are suitable for *your* iron condor. There is no single 'best' position that suits all traders.

--Ideas on how to manage risk.

--Figuring out when to exit. We'll discuss the pros and cons of locking in profits quickly (not a good idea) vs. holding longer (but not too long).

There is more that makes this book so special. It is not just a "how to" book. I share lessons that I've learned from a lifetime of trading options (starting in 1977 when I became a CBOE market maker). I share my philosophy on iron condor trading and ideas on how a winning trader thinks. The goal is to offer guidance that allows you to develop good trade habits and to avoid falling into easy-to-adopt poor habits. We all learn more about trading as we gain experience, but some mindsets are dangerous to your longevity as a trader and it is best to avoid developing those mindsets because they are so difficult to break.

To you, the reader

This book was prepared for an audience that already understands the most basic concepts about options. Although some of the material is suitable for rookies, if you do not understand the difference between a put and call or lack any experience trading options, I encourage you begin with the most basic concepts about options before continuing. There are numerous sources of information, but I recommend my recently updated (2013) "The Rookie's Guide to Options, 2nd edition."

My basic tenets

The following points represent the foundation of my beliefs, and the book is written accordingly:

--The ability to manage risk is the most important skill for any trader. Those who close their eyes hoping for a good outcome are destined to fail.

--If you have no knowledge of the 'Greeks,' you can still get much out of this book. However, it is mandatory for your long-term success as an option trader that you take time to undertake at least an elementary study of the Greeks. Understanding the Greeks is not difficult, despite what you probably believe, and it allows you to recognize the risk (and reward) potential for any position. But most of all, it ensures that you avoid owning a position (or portfolio) that could — in a worst case scenario — result in losing more money than you can afford.

--Trading without knowledge of how the Greeks work places a trader at a tremendous disadvantage.

--Discipline is necessary when managing risk. It is one thing to say that you understand what risk management is all about, but it is another to put it into practice. It is emotionally difficult to pull the trigger on necessary trades (that reduce risk) because most of the time such action involves locking in a loss.

--Let another trader earn the last nickel or dime on the position. Be willing to pay a small sum to exit the position, lock in profits, and eliminate all risk.

Other thoughts on iron condors

--There is often disagreement among traders and brokerage firms about what it means to 'buy' or 'sell' an iron condor. There is a solid rationale for using either term when making the trade, and there is no need to rehash the arguments here. I prefer the term 'buy' but will avoid using either term when discussing the trades.

However, you must know what "buy (or sell) an iron condor" means to your broker so that you can enter orders correctly.

--The iron condor is most often *traded* as a single transaction, consisting of four legs. That is how I encourage you to enter your orders because it is more efficient. However, it is reasonable for the more experienced trader to build the position with two separate trades (sale of call or put spread; followed by sale of the other spread). **NOTE** that selling the call and spreads separately is more difficulty than it appears, and I recommend against trading this way.

--The iron condor is *managed* as if it were two positions. This is not a contradiction. An adjustment is made when one of these two spreads is at risk of losing money much more rapidly than the other spread can earn money to offset that loss.

   --Short one call spread.

   --Short one put spread.

   --Seldom (if ever) hold positions all the way to expiration. It is usually not worth the risk required to seek every possible penny of profit.

It is easy to generate profits when trading iron condors because, under normal market conditions, traders earn a profit on a majority of their trades. The trade is initiated to produce a profit most of the time (perhaps 80 to 90+%).

HOWEVER, when losses are allowed to grow (i.e., risk is ignored), it becomes extremely difficult for any iron-condor trader to earn money over the longer term. The key is to manage risk so that no single loss wipes out too many profitable trades. When the trade is expected to be profitable 90% of the time, that means that a loss should be expected approximately one trade per ten. If that loss is allowed to reach its maximum theoretical amount, then it will be more than enough to erase the profits from the other nine winning trades.

--Using this strategy only during appropriate market conditions is essential. A strongly trending market usually leads to losses. Volatile markets are more difficult to manage, and I encourage you to avoid volatile markets until you have enough experience to feel comfortable when managing risk.

--Failure to recognize when a position has become too risky *for you* to hold, leads to large losses.

--Failure to take immediate action once you realize that risk of loss is imminent is likely to lead to realizing those losses. Sure, part of the time the losses never occur. But it is not reasonable to gamble.

This strategy is far from perfect, but is worth your time and effort to learn how to trade. It is *one* of the basic strategies that belong in your arsenal of trading ideas. Do not expect to use it as your only strategy.

As a reminder, this strategy is most effective when the trader has a market-neutral bias. If you prefer to own positions that prosper during a bullish or bearish market, the iron condor is not a good choice.

NOTE: Chapter one accommodates the needs of traders who are brand new to options. After that, the text assumes that readers already possess basic options knowledge.

Part I

Background Information &
General Ideas about Trading

Chapter 1

Some of the Finer Points

It is not difficult to learn the basic steps involved with setting up and trading an iron condor. This book teaches you to do that, and does so in great detail. However, because that information is available elsewhere, the major difference between this Iron Condor book and others is that the primary focus is on teaching readers to *understand* what they are doing, and how to make intelligent decisions.

When performing a variety of necessary tasks, we do the best we can. We think things through, make decisions and act on those decisions. Trading is different because it is a voluntary activity. If we cannot do the job effectively (profitably) then we do not have to spend our time and effort making trade/investment decisions. Instead we can turn our money over to professionals (index funds, financial planners, etc.) and let them do their thing.

Because you and I *choose* to use options and other investment vehicles actively, we should want to gather enough information to do so wisely. It makes sense to begin with the basics, and then – with a solid background behind us – move onto more advanced material. We want to make good decisions and trade in an intelligent manner. If we do that, our trading should be profitable. If we cannot outperform those who invest in index funds, there is no real purpose in trading. We can use our time to pursue a hobby.

Most hobbies cost money in exchange for the enjoyment they bring. However, investing and trading are not hobbies. They are serious undertakings. If you cannot take the time to learn how to use options to improve your financial well-being, then I urge you not to get involved. Trading is a serious business for serious people.

To that end, I share the thoughts of an experienced trader with the hope that you will gain an excellent understanding of the overall iron condor strategy. There is a significant difference between being able to mechanically make the trades and having the ability to make good (getting sufficient reward potential for the risk being taken) decisions. Although this book can be read by traders who are fairly new to options and have some trading experience, it is not intended to be your introduction to options.

Some of the ideas stressed in this book are:

--When it makes sense to trade iron condors and when it does not.

--The importance of managing risk. The sum at risk must never be large enough to demolish your portfolio. You can recover from losses, but it is impossible for most traders to come back from ruin.

--The feasibility of allowing the options to expire worthless and thereby seeking the maximum profit (holding to expiration) vs. exiting early to lock in profits and eliminate risk.

--Understanding why some positions are equivalent to others and that it truly makes no difference which of those 'essentially identical positions' you decide to trade.

--The importance portfolio cleansing where you eliminate any position that makes you nervous. Trading requires making winning decisions and accepting risk (there is no reward without some risk or everyone would be a trader). However, taking that risk must not leave you being uncomfortable or result in lost sleep because *nervous traders make rash decisions.*

--The desirability of owning iron condor positions with a relatively narrow spread width (defined as the difference in the strike prices between the two calls—or the two puts). In other words, do not own wide iron condors without a good reason.

--Believing that the iron condor is a single position, consisting of four legs. It is constructed by selling one call spread and one put spread on the same underlying asset. All options expire at the same time.

> *The trader's objective is to earn a profit on the whole iron condor. It is not to seek a profit from the call spread and another from the put spread.*

--Understanding that it is far more efficient to manage the iron condor as if it were two positions (call spread and put spread), but that your profit objective is based on owning a single position. Do not ignore the call spread to grab a quick profit on the put spread. This is a 'must-be-understood' concept.

--The importance of managing risk (there is no limit as to how often this should be repeated).

--Etc. There are many ideas that I share with readers, each of which is intended to make the overall trade plan successful. We do get to the specifics of trading, but I encourage you to have patience and read this book chapter by chapter. It is possible for you to develop difficult-to-break losing habits by getting started too quickly. One of the well-understood facts about traders is that discipline is difficult to maintain and bad habits are very difficult to break (because it may never occur to the trader that his standard operating procedure is flawed).

Do not get the idea that I am preaching. I sincerely want to share some of the lessons I learned over the past (almost) 40 years. There is no reason for each trader to make the same mistakes when they can be avoided.

Chapter 2

The Iron Condor

Terminology

To avoid any possible misunderstanding, let's clarify some terminology.

A **vertical spread** consists of two calls or two puts. Both options expire at the same time and are on the same underlying asset. When both options are calls, it is a **call spread**. If both options are puts, it is a **put spread**.

Example

> The following is a vertical spread. It is also a call spread. The last day of trading for both options is Nov 21, 2014. Although the true expiration date for those options is the following day, Saturday, Nov 22, 2014, we will use the customary terminology and refer to Nov 21 as either 'expiration day' or 'expiration Friday.'
>
> Buy 10 XYZ Nov 21 '14 110 calls
> Sell 10 XYZ Nov 21 '14 120 calls

When **buying a spread**, you buy the higher priced option (the option with the larger delta. Delta is one of 'the Greeks') and sell the lower priced option. For that reason, buying a spread always result in the expenditure of cash. Thus, when buying a vertical spread, the trade may be referred to as buying a **debit spread**.

Example

Consider the spread in the above example. The trader who makes both transactions *buys* the *debit* spread.

For clarification, and to use all of our descriptive words: If you make the trades indicated, you are *buying* 10-lots of the XYZ Nov 21, 2014 110/120 *call spread*. This is a *vertical spread* because the options expire at the same time and it is a *debit spread* because the 110 calls are more expensive than the 120 calls.

When **selling a spread**, you buy the less expensive option and sell the more costly option. This is a **credit spread** because cash is collected when the trade is made.

Examples

Buy 4 OFR Jul 18 '14 65 calls
Sell 4 OFR Jul 18 '14 60 calls

Buy 4 OFR Jul 18 '14 50 puts
Sell 4 OFR Jul 18 '14 55 puts

These two spreads have been sold. Each is a vertical spread. Each is a credit spread. The first is the OFR Jul 18, 2014 60/65 call spread and the other is the OFR Jul 18, 2014 50/55 put spread.

The trader who entered these orders (the orders were filled) collected cash when selling the call spread and collected more cash when selling the put spread.

NOTE: There is a big difference between 'collecting cash' when the trade is made and earning a profit. At some point in the future (no later than expiration day) the trader must buy the spread(s) just sold. When selling a spread, the trader earns a profit only when it can be bought at a price lower than the original sale price. Part of the time, both options in the credit spread **expire worthless** and the trader gets to keep every penny (minus commissions) of the original sale price.

The iron condor

When the trade consists of the sale of one call spread and one put spread – as in the above example using the two OFR spreads – and when the following are true, the position is a typical iron condor:

--When both spreads expire at the same time.

--The call and put options that were sold

　　--Have similar Deltas or

　　--Are roughly equally as far out of the money

--When the underlying asset is identical for each spread.

--When an equal quantity of each spread is sold (4-lots, in this example).

--When **the spread width** is identical.

　　--The spread width is the difference between the strike prices of the options that comprise the spread.

　　　　--The call spread width is five; (65 – 60)

　　　　--The put spread with is five; (55 – 50)

　　NOTE: Those are the only strike prices that matter. The difference between the put and call strike prices is immaterial. In fact, as long as that difference is not zero (i.e., as long as the short put spread and the short call spread do not have one strike price in common) the position is an iron condor. When they do have a common strike, then the position is an **iron butterfly**.

　　　Example of an iron butterfly:

　　　Buy 2 XYX Oct 60 puts
　　　Sell 2 XYX Oct 65 puts

　　　Sell 2 XYZ Oct 65 calls
　　　Buy 2 XYZ Oct 70 calls

Those are the requirements for a position to be an iron condor. However, it is very important for every reader to understand that you are free to trade any position that suits your needs. In this book, I write about true iron condors (i.e., positions that meet the above requirements), however, you may construct your position differently. Keep in mind that such minor changes may affect the name of the position that you own, but it should not have any effect on how you think about making the trade and managing risk.

TIPS for the thinking trader:
When you have a good reason to modify the iron condor, you may choose one of these ideas (or use your imagination):

--Sell more call spreads than put spreads; Sell more put spreads than call spreads. This adds a bearish or bullish bias to the position.

--One of the spreads is farther out of the money than the other. This adds a bearish or bullish bias to the position.

--Use different expiration dates for the call and put spreads.

When making the trades, it is common for traders to open the entire position in a single order. I encourage you to adopt that method. However, there is nothing wrong with 'legging'* into the position.

*Legging refers to trading part of the planned position first, and then trading the other part at a later time. Legging into iron condors is often done ineffectively, and I discourage adopting this technique.

Before discussing ideas on how to enter the trade, adjust the position when necessary, and make the all-important decision of when to exit the iron condor (to lock in a profit, reduce risk, or take a loss) let's look at some of the ideas about iron-condors that most writers never bother to mention.

Chapter 3

The Winning Iron Condor Mindset

All traders are most interested in learning the basic ideas about how to initiate the trade. That is typical human nature. You cannot earn money without trading, thus (the common thought goes) learning how to initiate trades becomes the overriding objective for any new trader.

I believe that learning to manage risk is far more important to your future financial success than learning how to open positions. Thus, risk management is not a topic you can ignore. In an effort to present the iron condor story in a logical sequence much of our discussion about managing risk must wait until you learn how to construct and trade an iron condor.

Before learning how and why a trader opens an iron condor position, let's look at some special thought patterns (what I refer to as a trader's mindset) that can help you have a better understanding of the subtleties of iron-condor trading.

I encourage you not to skip this material. If it does not make sense at this time (because you do not yet have a good feel for how iron condors work) then it will certainly make sense later. However, just being aware of these concepts at the very start of your iron condor education will help get you started on the right track. Avoiding mistakes is an essential part of any trader's education.

For readers who understand the basics of iron-condor trading, this material is likely to present thoughts that may not have occurred to you. I'm offering these thoughts upfront, rather than later, to help you avoid developing poor habits.

Thought #1: There is more than one way to manage an iron condor

Any position that meets the requirements listed in the previous chapter is an iron condor. Positions that are slightly modified may not be 'true' iron condors, but they should be managed as if they were. In other words, if you elect to sell five call spreads and six put spreads, the everyday risk-management decisions are the same as if it were a true 5-lot iron condor.

For discussion purposes (see below) I recommend classifying iron condors into four separate categories because the specific risk management techniques used are significantly different for each category. We'll take a closer look at that when we discuss how to manage iron condor positions. But for now, the material is presented as if all iron condors were created equal.

To be certain that we are all on the same wavelength, let's assume that we are referring to iron condors where

--The underlying asset is an index, rather than an individual stock.

--The index price is much higher than that of typical stocks, perhaps 1,000 to 3,000. Examples include SPX (the S&P 500 Index trading near 1,900); RUT (Russell 2000 Index, trading near 1,200); NDX (Nasdaq 100 index (3,800).

--The spread width is 10-points and the maximum possible loss for a one-lot iron condor position is $1,000, minus the premium collected.

--When trading an iron condor, you *sell* one call spread and *sell* one put spread, and always collect a cash premium when opening the position. Thus, the iron condor consists of two credit spreads. There is no discussion in this book about the opposite strategy which consists of buying two debit spreads. We make trades of that kind only when exiting our iron condors.

Thought #2: Different iron condor types:

--**Far OTM, very small premium, iron condors**. These are popular among some traders because money is earned (too little, in my opinion) in the vast majority of the trades. However, when losses do occur they are often large enough to wipe out years' worth of profits. I urge you not to trade this type of iron condor.

--All four options in the iron condor (IC) are reasonably far out of the money and have a low delta (less than 3).

--The premium available when selling the call and put spreads is small, perhaps $0.05 to $0.15 each. Thus, the profit potential is small.

--The probability (at the time when the trade is made) that all options will expire worthless (resulting in a profit) is 94% or higher.

--**Close-to-the-money (CTM) iron condors**. Because 'close to the money' is a relative term and is defined differently by each trader, for the purposes of this discussion I'm defining CTM options as those with a delta* of 20 to 35.

NOTE: The delta* refers to *the delta of the option sold* because that is the specific option that represents your risk. If that option moves into the money, or threatens to move into the money, the position will probably be underwater (losing money) and have become uncomfortable to hold (the probability of incurring additional losses is high). The option bought is of less importance in the overall scheme of things, because its sole purpose is to limit risk.

--Please do not think of the option bought as an income source. If this option is worth more than you paid for it, that is not a good sign. Why? Because the option sold always gains value more quickly than the option bought. In other words, when this options gain value, that is bad for the iron condor owner. Profits are earned when all options lose value over time.

--The premium generated is high, allowing for the chance to earn a very significant profit. For the 10-point iron condor, the premium can be $300 to $450. The actual premium collected depends on various factors:

--Real market conditions (especially volatility).

--Time until the options expire.

--Strike prices chosen (higher delta options offer higher premium).

--**Traditional iron condors**. This refers to the typical iron condor chosen by the vast majority of traders. There is no specific set of guidelines to establish a definition for a traditional iron condor (but we will discuss some good choices for newer traders later in this book), because the iron condor trader must:

--Be comfortable with the risk of owning the position.

--Be willing to accept that risk when seeking the available reward.

--Believe that the underlying index is likely to trade in a narrow price range (between the strike prices of the options sold) during the lifetime of the options.

--**Very short-term iron condors**. These are positions that expire in one or two weeks. Time decay is rapid (good for the trader), but negative gamma (another of the Greeks) presents high risk for the trader). It does not take much of a price change in the underlying asset to result in a loss.

Why be concerned with different types of iron condors?

--Each of these iron condors requires a slightly different way of thinking when it comes to managing the position.

--The wider the variety of iron condors available for trading, the better your chances of discovering the one or two that are best suited to your personal investing style and tolerance for risk.

-- However, it is too early to be concerned with the specific types. Just be aware there are plenty of iron condor varieties.

Thought #3: The iron condor is one position

The iron condor is one, and only one, position. For some traders this is a difficult concept to grasp. If may seem logical to think of the position as consisting of two credit spreads. The problem with that way of thinking is that it often results in poor risk-management decisions.

Example

You created an iron condor by

--Selling one call spread and collecting a premium of $1.20

--Selling one put spread and collecting $1.10

Bottom line: You traded one iron condor and collected $2.30. Let's say that a few days pass and the underlying index has moved higher. The call spread is worth $2.00 and the put spread is worth $0.60. You are losing money at this point because you must pay $2.60 to exit and that is $0.30 more than you collected to make the trade.

We will discuss how to handle the 'what should you do now' decisions later, but for now the vast majority of iron condor traders would (correctly) do nothing and hold the position as it exists.

The inexperienced trader who looks at the iron condor as two positions could easily believe that there is a $0.60 profit on the call spread. Because that represents 50% of the maximum possible profit from selling the call spread, this trader is tempted to buy (to close the position) the call spread, thereby locking in the $60 profit. This is a big mistake and something that the successful iron condor trader must learn to avoid.

> **FACT:** There is no $60 profit. The position is currently losing $30.
>
> If you can look at the iron condor position from this perspective; if you understand that there is no profit; then you have gone a long way towards understanding how to manage the position.

The key takeaway from this section is described by combining the following thoughts:

--The iron condor is a single position containing four different options.

--The call spread is not sold as an income source. It is sold as a hedge against being short the put spread. You do not make money by covering (closing or exiting) the call spread at less than you originally received.

--The put spread is not sold as an income source. It is sold as a hedge against being short the call spread. You do not make money by covering the put spread at less than you originally received.

--You sell *both* spreads as a single income source. You earn profits by closing the *whole iron condor* and paying a smaller premium than you collected when making the trade.

Thought #4: How the Iron Condor Traders Earn Money

The iron condor earns money when either or both of the following occur:

--Time passes and the underlying asset does not threaten to move past the strike price of the options you sold.

--Implied volatility declines, decreasing the value of both puts and calls.

Once the iron condor loses value and can be purchased at less than the premium collected, the trade can be closed at a profit. More detail in the next chapter.

Chapter 4

Iron Condor Theory & One Trading Rule

Once the underlying has been selected, the crucial decisions remain. Consider the following bullet points to be introductory statements with details to follow.

Finding an iron condor position:

--Which calls and puts should be sold?

NOTE: Choosing the spread to sell is the ultimate objective, but picking the option to sell is truly the important part of the trade.

--What is the proper spread width?

--It may seem 'obvious' that a trader should select the specific option to buy just as carefully as he/she chose which option to sell. However, that is not true. The most efficient method for trading iron condors (or selling credit spreads in general) is to select the spread width (which defines both options).

-- Finding an appropriate expiration date

--Short-term (1-2 weeks) options have to be handled differently than longer-term (2-3 months) iron condors. Therefore some discussion (next chapter) must be reserved for selecting an appropriate expiration date.

Iron Condor Theory

When trading an iron condor, we expect time to pass and the market to be non-volatile. If that is not the stock market that you expect to see, then it is the wrong time to trade iron condors.

When our expectations come true, it becomes profitable to close the position.

NOTE: If time passes, and the underlying price remains reasonably constant, then either the call spread or the put spread, *or both* lose value. This happens because the value of OTM options approaches zero as expiration nears, unless the strike price of the short option (of the call or put spread) is threatened (significant chance that the option will be ITM).

As time passes and expiration day draws closer, the chances of the underlying being able to make that move declines. Thus, the value of the options must decline.

  I hope it is understood that the spread loses value because the more expensive option (the one you sold) loses value more quickly (it has a higher theta) than the option owned. That shrinks the value of the call and put spreads, resulting in a profit.

At some point, the trader accepts the profit and exits. The general idea is: Time passes, nothing bad happens to the price of the underlying stock or index, and the trader earns a profit.

Of course it does not always work that way. When the underlying does undergo a significant price change, then the trader may decide to exit the position, even though it involves locking in a loss. That is done to prevent a larger loss. The rest of this discussion is withheld until we talk about risk management in Chapters 17-18.

General thoughts
The option spreads that you sell are out of the money (OTM) and you want them to remain OTM. The best way to achieve that goal is to sell options that are far OTM.

  --However, it is not that simple because the maximum possible profit is the cash collected from selling the call and put spreads.

    --When the spread is too far OTM, the premium is small.

--When the premium is too small, the potential profit is often insufficient to justify taking the risk necessary to earn the profit.

These two ideas are in conflict with each other.

You do want a high probability of earning a profit. However, this trade involves risk and there is no point in taking that risk when the reward is too small.

As you trade more iron condors you will get a good feel for a both the minimum acceptable premium —one that suits your trading style—and a desirable delta for your options being sold. (**NOTE**: Smaller delta options are farther out of the money). But for now, let's assume that we will not accept less than $0.40* for a 10-point call spread or a 10-point put spread on an index.

   * A guideline, not a rule. Some traders do settle for less. There is nothing wrong with that for the right trader.

Therefore, when selecting an iron condor to trade, there is always a trade-off, or compromise. You want some flexibility and do not want to be trapped into a set of rules that is uncomfortable for you, so let's begin with this rule:

My trading rule:
I believe that discipline in necessary for success, but am not a big fan of ironclad trading rules because a little flexibility is desirable. However, I do believe traders should adopt this rule:

> *If it is uncomfortable — for any reason — to own a specific position, then do not own it.*

This may seem trivial, but you would be surprised by how many people feel that they are 'forced' into holding a position for the simple reason that they are unwilling to exit a trade that would result in a loss.

This is destructive thinking. Please take my word for it: You will have many losing trades when trading this, or any option strategy. Your financial success as a trader does not depend on how many losing trades you have. Instead it is based on the size of those losing trades. More on this in Chapter 17.

--Getting out of the trade suggests that the original trade decision was a mistake, and traders do not like to admit to making mistakes.

--Believing that all losses result from mistakes is another destructive mindset. You must make the best decision you can make at the time a decision is needed. That is all you can do. Some decisions lead to profits and some lead to losses. Taking a loss does not mean that you made a mistake. It means that the decision did not work well *this time*. Remember that a decision that has a 95% probability of leading to success also means it will fail one time in 20. When that happens, the trader did not make a mistake.

--Do not be concerned with making mistakes. That is part of the learning process. Do be concerned if you make the same mistake repeatedly.

Your gut cannot predict where the stock market is headed, but if does express an opinion. When it makes you *nervous* to hold onto a trade, then please do not hold it. If it *frightens* you to hold onto a position, and you are too stubborn to exit, then I believe that your success as a trader is in serious doubt.

Preliminary risk-management lesson: When you make a decision that is good (right for you) at the time the decision is made, do not dwell on it. Do not track whether it was the winning or losing decision.

Trading involves living in the world of statistics. Much of the time, events occur as anticipated. But not always. There will be minor and major unexpected events in your life. Accept that as fact and do not beat yourself up over what you could have done differently. Live in the real world.

Chapter 5
Steady Monthly Income

One of the commonly accepted ideas about the iron condor is that it is an ideal strategy for generating a steady monthly income. Those who promote such ideas are doing a disservice to their readers. In my opinion, the truth is:

Iron condors can provide steady monthly income, but *only* when you, the trader, are:

--Disciplined and understand when to exit a losing trade.

--A skilled risk manager. The basic risk management skills taught in this book are sufficient for the newer trader. As with anything you learn in life, additional study can improve your skills. However, too many people believe that it is too difficult to understand risk management and they ignore this essential aspect of trading.

--Capable of adopting the strategy *only* at appropriate times. The primary rule is: this is not a bread-and-butter strategy and it should not be used every month.

--There will be times when the market is trending too hard in one direction or the other. Under those circumstances, iron condor traders soon discover that no call or put spread is far enough out of the money to allow the trader to hold onto the position and still remain within his/her comfort zone.

--When IV (implied volatility) is high, premium is high and that is a good time to trade iron condors. See Chapter 6.

--Not greedy I. You must understand that a few consecutive winning months is the norm and that obtaining such results has not turned you into a master iron condor trader.

--Not greedy II. Recognize when the residual profit potential is too small for the risk involved. Allow another trader to collect the last couple of nickels from the position.

--Not lazy. Do not expect to initiate trades, wait for time to pass, and then be allowed to exit with a good profit. Expect to work. Recognize that you may have to make many decisions (deciding to hold is a decision) over the lifetime of any given trade. It is true that you will find that some trades work perfectly, but many require your full attention.

Chapter 6

Trading Iron Condors in a Rising Volatility Environment

As mentioned, it is a good idea to trade iron condors when the implied volatility is high because the trader can collect a significantly higher cash premium than when IV is low. It is also true that a volatile market increases the odds that the market will move too far and require that you make an adjustment to avoid a large trading loss. However, the increased premium is often sufficient to compensate the trader for the extra risk.

When to take advantage of high IV: The winning plan

High IV is good for the iron condor trader, especially once it begins to level off and decline. That is when premium remains high despite the fact that the market has started to become less volatile.

Rising IV is not so good. Clarification: When you initiate an iron condor trade and IV continues to rise, that is likely to result in difficulty when it comes to managing the trade. Why? Because increasing IV means that the iron condor position premium is increasing – and your current trades would be underwater.

> **IMPORTANT NOTE**: It may be 'only' a paper loss because the trade has not yet been closed. But it is still a loss. Do not fall into the common trap of believing that there is no loss until a trade has been closed. When the net liquidation value of your brokerage account declines, you lost (past tense) money. When it increases, you earned money. As long as the position remains open, gains and losses come and go.

The rising IV vs. high IV statements may seem to be a contradiction, but it is not. For example, long-term average implied volatility (IV) for index options is roughly 20. When IV is 25, iron condor traders are pleased with the corresponding premium increase and begin to feel good about their positions. And they should.

However, when the markets are more volatile and when daily price swings are larger, it may be the beginning of a significant change in how traders feel about the future of the stock market. In other words, there is always the possibility that an increased demand for all options will drive IV higher. If you get excited (i.e., greedy) and double the size of your usual trade -- because IV increased to 30 from 20 -- you may soon discover that IV has zoomed past 50 and that you lost a lot of money from your newly-opened positions. Not only that, but losses are larger because you own larger positions. Worst of all is that IV is 50 and you may be forced out of your current positions, instead of being able to initiate new trades.

The best approach is to be patient and increase position size gently (by 10%, from 10-lots to 11- or perhaps 12-lots when IV reaches 25 and maybe another 10% when IV reaches 30). But beyond that, when IV continues to rise, you must be prepared – just in case this is one of those times when IV explodes and reaches extremely high levels (60 to 80). You cannot afford to own too many iron condors *during* that IV rise. It could literally put you out of business by destroying your trading account.

Thus, once you increased size by 10 to 20% during an initial IV increase, have the patience to wait until the data tells you that IV has topped and has begun to decrease before trading even more size. You may miss the best opportunity, but you will also have missed 100% of the opportunities to enter into a money-losing trade. When you see an apparent IV top, it is much safer to trade a few more spreads. But do not get greedy. Be aware of potential losses -- IV may rise again after a brief pause.

The moral of the story is simple to understand but almost impossible for the undisciplined trader to put into practice. When IV rises, it is time to consider trading iron condors. If you already own iron condors, it pays to be patient before you become more aggressive.

However, if market volatility and IV continue to rise, discontinue that aggressive streak. It is far better to wait, devoting your time to managing existing positions. The time to become aggressive is after IV appears to have reached its maximum; after IV has leveled and started to decrease. That spares you from the pain and suffering that comes with a large portfolio of iron condor positions in a rapidly rising IV environment.

There is no need to take extra risk unless you are truly prepared to do so. The whole point of using options as your primary trading tool is to minimize the sum of money at risk and to increase the probability of owning profitable trades. Just as with the stock market, your goal should never be to buy the bottom or sell the (IV) top. I urge you to construct a trade plan that describes 'earning money with appropriate risk' — and not 'earning the maximum possible amount' — as the objective.

Part II

Nuts & Bolts of Trading

Iron Condors

Introduction to Part II

In the following chapters I offer suggestions about a variety of items when designing the specific iron condor to trade.

There is a ton of material here, and much of it may be overwhelming to the person who is encountering options for the first time. As mentioned, those brand new option traders should not begin their education by learning about iron condors, especially when the discussions are targeted to traders who have some trading experience. It is far more important to get a solid foundation in the basic concepts before spending your time selecting which strategy to trade.

The objective in offering so much detail is to make it clear to every reader that trading is not as simple as:

--Step one: Initiate a trade

--Step two: Close the trade and bank the profits.

NOTE: It is not necessary to have a full understanding of each idea discussed before you begin trading. However, it is important to be aware of how many things a trader can consider when plying his/her trade. Use as few or as many of these ideas as makes you comfortable. Just be aware that no strategy is good enough for you to expect to earn money without a significant effort.

Suggestion: Read all of Part II to get an overview. Next, re-read more slowly to allow for a better understanding. Concentrate on chapters that deal with the top decisions:

Chapter 13; Choosing Strike Prices

Chapter 14; Choosing the Spread Width

Chapter 15; Choosing the Expiration

Chapter 16: When to Exit

Let's begin at the beginning and think about entering orders. One problem with trading options is that the bid/ask markets can be very wide (i.e., the ask price is much higher than the bid price) with many stock or index options. I offer suggestions on how to overcome this difficulty.

If you trade options where the bid and ask prices are very close to each other, then you will not have to be overly concerned with the contents of the next chapter.

Chapter 7

Navigating the Bid/Ask Spreads

In this chapter, I often use the phrase "option to sell." That *does not* suggest selling the specified option and then buying another option to complete the spread. Instead, that phrase encompasses all of the following:

--When trading iron condors, you sell one call spread and one put spread. For each of those spreads, the procedure is:

--First, choose which call or put option to sell.

--Second, choose which options to buy based only on the desired spread width. A complete discussion of spread width appears in Chapter 14.

--Third, enter an order to sell the call spread, the put spread, or both spreads simultaneously (that's the complete iron condor). Do not enter an order to buy or sell single options – only trade spreads.

The contents of this chapter will have a real influence on your results because they explain how NOT to give away your money.

Every time we make a trade, we lose money to slippage. That term refers to the fact that we are customers and not market makers and we pay prices nearer to the ask when buying options and collect a premium nearer to the bid when selling.

You can enter a bid at any price level, and there is a small (but finite) chance of getting filled at that price. This is true for both spreads and orders for single options. However,

> *When you want to buy a call option (or other bullish position) at a low price (near the bid), it is unusual to be filled at a time when you will be pleased.*
>
> *If the underlying asset price declines, then your 'low bid' for a bullish position may become the 'ask' price and your order would be filled at that time.*

The point of this discussion is that the customary price at which our orders are filled is a small amount worse than the midpoint (the price equally between the bid and ask prices). This 'small amount worse' represents the 'slippage.' Every time we trade, we give up some cash because of slippage.

One way for retail traders to deal with the difficulty of facing a wide bid/ask spread is to think about the option price as being the midpoint (i.e., average of the bid and ask prices) – and then being willing to pay a bit more (or accept a bit less) when trading. I define 'a bit' as five-cents. But it can be 10-cents when dealing with options priced above $2. This is far better than paying the ask price or selling at the bid price. It is typical for newer traders to fail to recognize that the markets are auction markets and that there is no need to pay the ask price when it is far above the bid price.

When your order is filled at that 'near-the-midpoint' price, you won't have that sinking feeling that you are already losing money on the trade.

Getting market quotes
--Always use live data. Never enter a live order when using delayed data. If you choose to look for trade possibilities when the markets are closed, please

recognize that prices may be VERY different when the market opens the following morning.

--Look at the market (bid and ask prices) for each option that you may want to trade as part of a spread. For example, see figure 8.1.

--Examine a variety of calls/puts. I encourage basing your decision on which options to trade according to the option delta. [If you are unfamiliar with the term 'delta' or 'the Greeks' in general, then you are not yet ready to trade iron condors (or almost any other strategy). Take a few minutes to understand what delta is and what it measures.]

When you are new to trading iron condors, it may be difficult to understand the rationale behind the suggestion to structure the call and put spreads such that the short option has a 10-delta (or 7 or 15 or any other value). The bottom line is that the experienced trader can look back on his/her trades and recognize that some trades were more profitable than others. When that data suggests that 10-delta options work better than 15-delta options, then the trader naturally tends to adopt the "10-delta iron condor" strategy.

Please understand that the above paragraph refers to a specific trader who exercises his preferences when managing the iron condor. If that trader finds that the 10-delta iron condor works for him, it does not mean it will work for you. We all have different skill sets, we all have different comfort zones and that means:

> There is no such thing as the "best" iron condor to trade.

Newer traders have work to do before they can have a good feel for choosing specific options to trade. The decision is based on your personal risk tolerance, profit objectives (aggressive vs. more conservative), and your ability to manage risk. Go with something that feels comfortable (i.e., you are not overly worried about losses from the position), trade small size, and get some trades under your belt.

--Suggestion for new traders when using index options: Sell option spreads for which the short option has a delta is between 6 and 9. Complete the spread based on your chosen spread width (Chapter 14).

--Discussions on the thought process behind choosing an appropriate delta occur frequently throughout the book.

Getting Market quotes for spreads

Some concepts will be 'obvious' once you begin trading spreads (call spreads, put spreads, or iron condors). That comes with experience. I include some of those concepts below to help you understand the concepts more quickly. That should translate into saving money.

I recommend (when trading high-priced index options, such as SPX) using spreads where the option bought is 10-points farther out of the money than the option sold. Alternative ideas are discussed in Chapter 14.

Once you have your list of options to sell, look at a bid/ask quote for the *specific spreads* (see figure 8.2, for example) that you may want to trade.

--Specific call spreads, as in figure 8.2.

--Specific put spreads (figure 8.2).

--The whole iron condor after you decide which call and put spreads to trade. No examples are illustrated.

Broker trading platform: If you do not know how to use your broker's trading platform to obtain current spread quotes, or to enter orders, call customer service and request instructions. Do not lose money by entering orders incorrectly. Practice using the platform until you know how to use it. Most platforms are easy to use, but others come with unexpected difficulties.

Plan to buy or sell an iron condor. Be very careful. My broker labels the trade as '*sell* an iron condor.' However, other brokers refer to this as a '*buy*.' To be certain you get it right:

--Set up a paper-trading account and make some trades. Then examine the positions and be certain you own the desired position. Don't get overconfident here because some broker platforms can be confusing.

--Be certain that cash was collected for the trade. When selling one call spread and selling one put spread, you collect cash.

--Be certain that you sold an option with a higher delta (than the option bought) for both the call and put spreads.

Look at the market quote for the iron condor. Determine the midpoint (of the bid and ask prices). If that price (premium) is too small and unacceptable, there is little you can do other than have patience or find a different iron condor to trade.

Once you find a potential trade, enter an order at a price that is 'five cents worse' than the midpoint. Because the iron condor is a credit spread and you are collecting cash, 'five cents worse' means that you are accepting $0.05 less than the midpoint price.

Example

An iron condor market is:

Bid: $1.20

Ask $2.00

Midpoint: $1.60

Enter your order to collect a credit of $1.55.

After some time passes, depending on the target price for the trade (and your patience to wait), you may have to lower your limit price by another five cents to 'ten cents worse than midpoint.' In this example that would be $1.50.

Be careful not to lower your price so many times that your execution price is no longer acceptable. No trade is so good that you can afford to accept any trade execution available. Always have a limit on how much you are willing to be paid to trade the iron condor.

Market conditions change over time and although you will get filled at 'ten cents under midpoint' often on some days, at other times you may have to go as far as 'twenty cents under.' Please know your true price limit and if you cannot make the trade at a price that works for you, it is better to skip the trade and try again the next day.

I suggest getting started by refusing to move more than 20 cents beyond the midpoint. As you make more trades, you can use your own judgment on where to set your minimum acceptable price.

It is easier to get an order filled when the underlying asset has options that are actively traded (high volume). SPX, NDX, RUT fill that bill. In addition, the ETFs based on those indexes are also very suitable for trading (SPY, QQQ, IWM).

NOTE: One SPY option is 1/10 as large as one SPX option, and the premium is also 1/10 as much, and the options have strikes that are 1-point apart. Please be sure that you understand: Ten 1-point SPY spreads is nearly the exact same trade as one 10-point SPX trade.

SPECIAL NOTE: SPY options trade with very narrow bid/ask spreads. If the bid/ask spread is 10-cents wide, that is equivalent to seeing a market that is $1 wide on an SPX option with the strike price that is 10x as large.

EXAMPLE

SPX quote: SPX Jul 1900 C: $14.50 bid/ $15.20 ask.

SPY Quote: SPY Jul 190 C: $1.45 bid/ $1.52 ask.

Although SPX does is not valued at exactly 10-times the value of SPY, they are close enough to make these points:

--Buying 10 SPY Jul 190 calls @ $1.49 is essentially the same as buying one SPX Jul 1900 call @ $14.90

--The SPX call has a midpoint of $14.85 and it is okay to bid 5 or 10 cents over that price. But:

The midpoint for the SPY option is $1.485. **DO NOT BID 5-CENTS OVER THAT PRICE**.

The recommended starting increment is one-half cent ($0.005) to one cent ($0.01). That translates to bidding $1.49,

---

Important NOTE: On many occasions, the bid/ask market quote is so wide that the bid for a spread can be less than zero. Please recognize that this quote is coming from a computer and not from a real person. Why is this important?

If you see a market quote for a spread that resembles:

Bid: $-0.80; Ask: $2.00; Midpoint: $0.60

The midpoint is not $0.60.

Always assume that the bid for any option or any spread is at least $0.00. Thus, the quote becomes $0 to $2 and the midpoint is $1.00. In fact, you could assume that the true bid is some low price, perhaps $0.20. That increases the true midpoint to $1.10.

If this is a spread that you want to sell, do not try to sell near the 'fake midpoint' of $0.60. Instead, use the more realistic midpoint of $1.00 or $1.10.

In this situation, never offer to sell your spread at $0.55. Begin with an asking price that is based on the true midpoint, $0.95 or $1.05 in this example.

Don't take shortcuts. The price at which you buy and sell does make a difference in your long-term results. Look at the quotes for the individual options and also the quotes for the specific spreads of interest. In some instances, the spread quote will be more favorable than the quotes for the individual options.

Once again, a crucial point is that you must ignore all bids below zero. This is not a trivial matter. It is likely that your broker's midpoint calculator does not take this precautionary step.

I understand that you are anxious to begin. And it is acceptable to take a little less premium on any given trade — but only as tuition cost for an education. Do not get into the habit of forcing trades.

One additional subtle point
When you look at the quote for the spread, be certain that the quote is based on the quotes for the individual options; otherwise the midpoint may be unrealistic.

Example: Selling a call spread

Market for call that you plan to sell: $3.00 to $3.60 (Note this abbreviated format for a bid/ask quote. The bid price always comes first and is smaller than the ask price.)

Market price for the option you plan to buy: $2.10 to $2.60

--The bid is $3.00 minus $2.60

--The ask is $3.60 minus $2.10

Theoretical (extra wide) bid/ask quote for the spread: $0.40 to $1.50. That makes the spread midpoint $0.95.

However the quote for the spread could be: $.40 to 1.00 because someone is trying to make the same trade as you, i.e., selling the spread. That person is offering to sell at $1.00, making the midpoint appear to be $0.70 when it is really $0.95.

Thus your sale price should be based on the wide market ($0.40 to $1.50; midpoint $0.95 and not on the 'apparent spread quote' of $0.40 to $1.00; midpoint $0.70). If you end up selling such spreads at $0.65 instead of $0.90, it will be difficult to make money.

It may feel like a waste of time to verify the 'true' spread quote, but it is not. Wide bid/ask spreads can kill any trader's ability to earn money. Therefore, it is essential to understand the markets to avoid paying too much or accepting too little for any trade.

It is almost never necessary to take immediate action and you can afford to try one price — even for as little as a few seconds — before sacrificing another five or ten cents.

If you accept the cautions mentioned in this chapter, you will save yourself a lot of trading over the years. It is far too easy to let success blind you to the necessity of not tossing cash into the trash. Be careful when entering orders.

Chapter 8

Trade Screens

Many discussions in the book use the numbers that come from figures 8.1 and 8.2.

Live data; 1/24/2014 10:15am CT
RUT: 1148.35 bid/ 1148.40 ask

Figure 8.1: RUT Put and Call Options

Undr...	Description	Nt Pc / Ac Ac	Bd Sz / TIF	Bid	Ask	Ask	Last	Mid	Cl	Impld Vl. %	OI	Delta
	Feb 20, 2104 PUTS											
RUT	Index						1148.35				606K	
RUT	FEB 20 '14 1010 Put		53	1.80	1.95	86	1.45	1.88		28.595%	3.35K	-0.0472
RUT	FEB 20 '14 1020 Put		51	2.10	2.25	135	2.10	2.18		27.691%	5.62K	-0.0554
RUT	FEB 20 '14 1030 Put		55	2.45	2.60	112	2.00	2.53		26.769%	6.62K	-0.0650
RUT	FEB 20 '14 1040 Put		58	2.85	3.00	83	2.85	2.92		25.806%	6.33K	-0.0763
RUT	FEB 20 '14 1050 Put		180	3.30	3.50	32	3.40	3.40		24.983%	7.85K	-0.0909
RUT	FEB 20 '14 1060 Put		18	4.00	4.20	84	4.00	4.10		24.046%	9.98K	-0.1075
RUT	FEB 20 '14 1070 Put		156	4.70	5.00	161	4.90	4.85		23.374%	7.36K	-0.1300
RUT	FEB 20 '14 1080 Put		124	5.60	6.00	174	5.70	5.80		22.298%	7.26K	-0.1527
RUT	FEB 20 '14 1090 Put		86	6.80	7.20	139	6.90	7.00		21.498%	4.17K	-0.1830
RUT	FEB 20 '14 1100 Put		114	8.30	8.70	86	8.40	8.50		20.732%	3.92K	-0.2195
RUT	FEB 20 '14 1170 Call		317	9.50	10.30	151	10.20	9.90		15.411%	3.15K	0.3291
RUT	FEB 20 '14 1180 Call		325	6.10	7.00	158	7.20	6.55		15.008%	3.44K	0.2536
RUT	FEB 20 '14 1190 Call		255	3.80	4.40	139	4.60	4.10		14.416%	2.29K	0.1823
RUT	FEB 20 '14 1200 Call		122	2.25	2.50	62	2.50	2.38		13.748%	3.44K	0.1199
RUT	FEB 20 '14 1210 Call		97	1.20	1.50	117	1.45	1.35		13.494%	7.36K	0.0773
RUT	FEB 20 '14 1220 Call		95	0.60	0.80	147	0.70	0.70		12.945%	8.20K	0.0429

Figure 8.2: RUT Put and Call 10-point Spreads

Undr...	Description	Nt Pc / Ac Ac	Bd Sz / TIF	Bid / Quantity	Ask / Destination	Ask / Stts	Last / Lmt Price	Mid / Type	Cl	Impld Vl. %	OI	Delta
RUT	Index						1148.40				606K	
RUT	FEB 20 '14 - 1010 + 1020 Put		46	0.15	0.28	1	0.25	0.22				
RUT	FEB 20 '14 - 1020 + 1030 Put		72	0.20	0.40	8	0.35	0.30				
RUT	FEB 20 '14 - 1030 + 1040 Put		2	0.35	0.55	5	0.40	0.45				
RUT	FEB 20 '14 - 1040 + 1050 Put		5	0.30	0.50	20	0.47	0.40				
RUT	FEB 20 '14 - 1050 + 1060 Put		151	0.30	0.60	3	0.57	0.45				
RUT	FEB 20 '14 - 1060 + 1070 Put		82	0.50	1.00	15	0.70	0.75				
RUT	FEB 20 '14 - 1070 + 1080 Put		105	0.60	1.00	10	0.70	0.80				
RUT	FEB 20 '14 - 1080 + 1090 Put		166	0.80	1.20	5	1.10	1.00				
RUT	FEB 20 '14 - 1090 + 1100 Put		71	1.10	1.90	74	1.47	1.50				
RUT	FEB 20 '14 + 1170 - 1180 Call		221	2.50	4.00	1	4.00	3.25				
RUT	FEB 20 '14 + 1180 - 1190 Call		184	1.70	3.20	138	3.31	2.45				
RUT	FEB 20 '14 + 1190 - 1200 Call		120	1.30	2.20	176	2.00	1.75				
RUT	FEB 20 '14 + 1200 - 1210 Call		1	0.85	1.15	20	1.00	1.00				
RUT	FEB 20 '14 + 1210 - 1220 Call		20	0.45	0.75	7	0.70	0.60				

Chapter 9

Items to Consider when Making the Trade

As you gain trading experience, the time required for decision making decreases because some decisions (choosing an expiration date, for example) become semi-automatic. The more difficult decisions (adjust vs. exit) require less time because your experience allows the thought process to become more efficient.

When beginning, you may want to consider constructing the iron condor from a wide variety of options. However, once you go through the process once or twice, you will automatically recognize that many of the calls and puts can be eliminated from consideration. For example, the option's delta, strike price, or premium will be outside the range of acceptable (for you) choices.

Iron condor traders tend to trade far out-of-the-money options, but not so far that the premium is too small to offer much profit potential. Once you trade an iron condor for a specific underlying asset, you will have a good clue as to where to begin the selection process next time.

EXAMPLE: for a 10-point, index iron condor

As a new iron-condor trader, I recommend choosing options whose deltas range between 6 and 9 (when trading index options). If you are an experienced iron condor trader, then you already have a decent understanding of which options are comfortable to trade and can afford to expand your option choice. I believe that experienced traders can trade options whose delta is between 5 and 15).

Eliminate all expiration dates longer than 4-months and shorter than 3-weeks. When brand new to iron condor trading, two-month options (eight or nine weeks) are a reasonable place to begin.

Eliminate call spreads and put spreads when the premium is less than a given minimum. I suggest choosing a minimum price between $0.25 and $0.40. **NOTE**: This is the lowest recommended minimum. It is very acceptable to choose a higher minimum premium. Remember that if you choose a $0.40 minimum for each spread, then the iron condor premium will be no less than $0.80.

Your personal comfort zone will butt in and convince you that selling certain options is too risky. Pay attention to that feeling. For trading experience to be *useful* (i.e., in order for the trader to learn something from owning and managing the position), he/she must be in control. When you are nervous or uncomfortable, it is difficult to make intelligent decisions. Let me assure you that fear of losing too much money is at the top of the list of situations that you MUST avoid.

Decisions

Each of us has our own way of thinking and something that may seem obvious to one person may be a mystery to another. So if you have questions, please ask [rookies (at) mdwoptions (dot) com.]

I hope you will come out of this discussion with a good feeling about your ability to make intelligent choices when building your first (or any) iron condor.

Let's get started by looking at the trading screens (figures 8.1 and 8.2). The data represents a fraction of the available choices (options are available with strike prices ranging from 600 to 1400). Eliminating options that are too far out of the money is one of those easy-to-make decisions.

We must look at the list of available choices and select some worthy of further consideration. For those with virtually no experience, I'll make recommendations. For experienced traders, ignore those suggestions and substitute your own.

> *My objective is to help everyone understand the selection process and it is not to make specific recommendations because market conditions change and our comfort zones change along with them.*

More importantly, sometime it pays to trade more conservatively than at other times. So there is never going to be a single 'best' iron condor choice that is suitable for everyone.

First we will look at the numbers and choose a put spread. Next, we'll look at the call spreads. In this chapter, the commentary is of a general nature because there is a lot of background that you, the trader, should understand before making trades with real money. The specifics begin in the following chapter.

The data presented in figure 8.1 show put options whose delta ranges from (we ignore the fact that puts have negative delta and only consider the absolute value of the delta) 5 to 22. The call deltas range from 4 to 33.

Fact: Implied volatility (IV) for equity options decreases as the strike price increases. This is known as volatility skew. Skew was not a factor in options pricing until after the market crash of October 1987. Since that time, market makers took into consideration the fact that markets may decline less often than they rally, but declines are often much more severe than the rallies. Thus, owning puts (along with a decrease in the number people who are willing to sell puts) became desirable – for protection, if not for speculation. That's just another way of saying that when the call and put are an equal number of points out of the money, the put options carry a higher implied volatility, and thus are priced higher. And that's the brief story on volatility skew.

Lower implied volatility for call options translates into option prices that say the following: As the market rises, there is a smaller chance that the underlying price will continue to rise -- and that in turn reduces the probability of the option being in the money when expiration arrives. Therefore, delta (a measure of the probability that an option will be in the money at expiration) is smaller for call options than it is for put options – when the options are equally far out of the money.

What does that mean for us when looking for spreads to trade? It means that call delta and call premium decline faster (compared with puts) as the option becomes farther out of the money. Translation: (a) call premium declines rapidly as we move farther OTM and quickly become too inexpensive to sell; (b) There may be only two or three viable call options to sell; puts offer a wider selection.

> **NOTE:** Do not become confused by option skew. It is obvious that the underlying asset is a single entity and when estimating its future volatility, there is only one best guess as to just how volatile any stock or index will be. However, market declines tend to be sharper and deeper than rallies and buyers of put options are willing to pay a higher premium than call buyers – for options that appear to have an equal chance (they are the same number of points OTM) of being in the money by expiration. Those higher prices translate into a higher implied volatility.

I chose a set of options (figure 8.1) for this conversation because the vast majority of iron condor traders would choose their options from this group.

Looking at the numbers, do not be overwhelmed by how much there is. Some of the numbers can be ignored. The especially important data are:

--The bid and ask quotes for each option (and the midpoint). Those numbers are important because they dictate the price at which the options can be bought and sold.

--The other very important piece of information is the option delta because it represents a good approximation of the probability that an option will be in the money when expiration arrives. When trading iron condors, profits are earned when time passes and the options neither move into the money, nor threaten to move into the money. Therefore low delta options provide a high probability of earning money on the trade. But if the probability (delta) is too low then the possible profit (premium) becomes too small for you to take the risk of earning that premium.

Traders often ignore the idea that delta can be used as a probability estimate. The primary definition of delta is: An excellent estimate for how much the price of the option changes when the underlying asset changes by one point.

If you are not comfortable selling a spread because the delta of the short option is too high (i.e., the chances of the option moving into the money make you fear the outcome), that is an important warning sign that cannot be ignored. I've said this before, but here it is again, using different words:

> ***Do not own any position that makes you afraid of potential loss.***
>
> ***It is far better to miss a profitable opportunity than to suffer anxiety.***

Traders who are afraid or uncomfortable tend to make bad decisions.

As intelligent investor/traders we do not want trade decisions to be the result of emotional thinking (especially fear or greed). Traders tend to be excited about possible profits, and that may allow greed to take charge of the decision-making process. On the other hand, when the potential loss is high – even when it is unlikely that the amount will be lost -- new traders tend to be overwhelmed with fear. When we construct positions and trade an appropriate number of spreads, then both fear and greed should be absent.

Learning to manage risk goes a long way towards helping you set up trades so that they are comfortable to own. Therefore it is important to think about how to manage risk at the very beginning of your trading career. This discussion is continued in Chapter 17.

The delta of the option being sold goes a long way towards giving the inexperienced trader a sense of how likely he/she is to make money from the position. And once you learn to appreciate the importance of delta, you may realize that for you, delta has become the most important characteristic of the options that you choose to sell.

If you already trade vertical (credit or debit) spreads, you should already have some experience thinking about delta when selecting your trades. That experience is beneficial to the iron condor trader.

I'll be referring to delta many times during the discussion on making trade decisions using the screen shots in figures 8.1 and 8.2.

Market Neutral
Iron condors begin life as market-neutral positions. That means the trader has neither a bullish nor bearish bias and the trade does not begin to earn or lose money when the underlying asset undergoes a small price change. For that reason, you cannot expect to use iron condors as your only option strategy, unless you never have a market opinion.

Let's assume that you believe the generally-offered advice of financial professionals: It is next-to impossible to time the stock market well enough to earn extra money and the best results (they say) are achieved by those who buy and hold.

The only portion of that advice of importance to us is the opinion of how difficult it is to know whether the market's next move will be up or down. If you accept that premise, then you will almost certainly want to trade with a market-neutral bias. The iron condor is a suitable strategy for such traders.

The truth is that most individual traders believe that such advice is nonsense and — despite evidence to the contrary. If you are in that group, I recommend using the iron condor only when your market prediction is neutral over the short term.

If you are in that group then I recommend using the iron condor only when your market prediction for the near-term is for the market to trade in a relatively narrow range.

When you have a strong bullish or bearish expectation, the iron condor is the wrong strategy. Instead, use one half of an iron condor. In other words, you can sell only put spreads when bullish and sell only call spreads when bearish. That means you would be trading credit spreads using calls or puts, but not both. Although there is an obvious similarity between credit spreads and iron condors, there are enough differences that you cannot apply everything in this book to the credit spread strategy.

What is market neutral?
The traditional definition of a market-neutral spread is one whose total delta is zero or near zero.

Here is a simple set of rules for calculating position delta:

--If you own an option, add its delta to the total. Remember that puts have negative delta, so if you own puts, subtract the absolute value of its delta from the total.

--If you are short (i.e., sold) any option, subtract its delta from the total.

--For each different option in the position multiply its delta by the number of contracts held.

--The sum is the position delta.

Example

What is the position delta for the following spread?

> Buy 6 XYZ Apr 150 puts; delta -.18
> Sell 6 XYZ Apr 160 puts; delta -.25

Answer:

You bought six Apr 150 puts and that position is short 18 * 6, or 108 deltas.

You sold six Apr 160 puts, so the position is long 25 * 6, or 150 deltas.

Position delta = -108 + 150; or +42 deltas

This is a bullish position (it has positive delta).

For various (appropriate) reasons, some traders find it more comfortable to own a position that is not delta neutral, but is market neutral from a different perspective.

EXAMPLE
"Neutral" iron condor positions

--Sell one call spread and one put spread such that the *total position delta* is zero. This is your typical delta-neutral position.

--Sell one call spread and one put spread such that the delta of the options sold are as near each other as possible. This method for constructing iron condors ignores the delta of the option that you buy. These iron condors tend to be delta short because of volatility skew. In other words, when considering only the options bought, the put options have a higher (negative) delta than the calls.

--Sell one call spread and one put spread such that the two short options are equally far out of the money.

54

Example

--With XYX currently trading near $180 per share, create an iron condor in which you sell the $170 put and $190 call, with both options expiring at the same time.

--Please understand that it often is impossible to choose equally far out-of-the-money options because options with the specific strike prices do not exist. Options trade with strike prices at specific and standardized increments. If the stock is $181, the best you can do is to sell the $190 call and $170 put because the $191 and $171 are not available.

--These equally-distant iron condor positions are delta long (due to volatility skew), and most option experts do not consider this position as market neutral. However, in my opinion, this is a viable plan for some traders.

--Another way to be market neutral is to be dollar neutral. In other words, sell one call spread and one put spread (of equal width) that are equally priced. Typically this choice is unavailable unless there are many different strike prices (high-priced index).

I recommend using delta-neutral positions when first getting started. However, if you cannot decide which 'neutral' is best for *your* trading, compromise is possible.

Example: XYZ is $600/share

The distance-neutral strategy calls for selling XYZ Dec 540 puts and Dec 660 calls.

The delta-neutral strategy calls for selling XYZ Dec 530 puts and XYZ Dec 650 calls.

Solution: Choose options with strike prices between those above. One possible iron condor is to sell XYZ Dec 535 puts and the Dec 655 calls. [535 is the average of 530 and 540; 655 is the average of 650 and 660.]

The point is that you may choose a 'neutral' iron condor that is neutral by any standard that you care to adopt.

Not quite market neutral

It is possible to trade positions that are 'almost' iron condors, but are constructed with a small market bias (or market fear). If you want to get fancy with any of those non-neutral positions, please learn how to trade the standard iron condor before trying to outsmart the system.

Example
--Sell an unequal number of put spreads and call spreads.

--Go farther out of the money when selling either the call or put spread.

--DO NOT choose spreads with different expirations because they are too difficult to manage.

--DO NOT choose spreads of unequal width unless you compensate for overall risk. If you sell ten 10-point put spreads SELL ONLY FIVE 20-point call spreads.

It's time to look at the specific options available for trading as we construct our iron condor position.

Chapter 10

The Put Spread

All put options have negative delta. In other words, the price of the put tends to decline as the underlying price rises. All calls have positive delta and tend to gain value when the underlying price rises. **Reminder:** Sometimes the effects of a substantial implied volatility change can override the effect of delta on the price of any option. Translation: If IV rises by enough, call options *could* gain value when the stock price falls.

An iron condor is one position with four legs. However, when deciding which options to include in our position, it is not reasonable to look at all four options simultaneously.

Thus, we choose either the put or call spread first and then the other.

About the numbers
The numbers represent real-world data from Jan 24, 2014. For the purpose of this example, options expire Feb 21, 2014, or 29 days from trade date.

NOTE: In the figures that follow, the options are designated as expiring Feb 20. Interactive Brokers (the source of the images) uses that date because it is the last day that these index options trade. Settlement for cash-settled, Europeans style RUT options is determined by the *opening prices* of each of the stocks in the index on Friday morning, Feb 21.

Figures 8.1 and 8.2 represent a typical set of live data. For the given expiration date, there are options with many additional strike prices from which you can choose. However, as I will make clear, there is no reason for most of us to care about options that were omitted.

The following text describes how I go about making trade decisions. I've included extra explanatory comments because the idea is to provide insight on how the decision process may work for you. My objective is to make it less complicated to trade iron condors and to help you weave your way efficiently through the maze of possible positions to find one that is appropriate for you.

One point: Your actual thoughts (real time) will become much more streamlined —once you manage a few trades. If I include too much detail, please understand that it is intended to benefit the less-experienced trader.

The put spread sale

Figure 8.1 is reproduced for convenience.

Undr...	Description	Nt Pc	Bd Sz	Bid	Ask	Ask	Last	Mid	Cl	Impld Vl. %	OI	Delta
		Ac Ac	TIF			Stts	Lmt Price					
Feb 20, 2104 PUTS												
RUT	Index						1148.35				606K	
RUT	FEB 20 '14 1010 Put	53	1.80	1.95 •	86		1.45	1.88		28.595%	3.35K	-0.0472
RUT	FEB 20 '14 1020 Put	51	2.10	2.25	135		2.10	2.18		27.691%	5.62K	-0.0554
RUT	FEB 20 '14 1030 Put	55 •	2.45	2.60	112		2.00	2.53		26.769%	6.62K	-0.0650
RUT	FEB 20 '14 1040 Put	58	2.85	3.00	83		2.85	2.92		25.806%	6.33K	-0.0763
RUT	FEB 20 '14 1050 Put	180	3.30	3.50 •	32		3.40	3.40		24.983%	7.85K	-0.0909
RUT	FEB 20 '14 1060 Put	18	4.00	4.20	84		4.00	4.10		24.046%	9.98K	-0.1075
RUT	FEB 20 '14 1070 Put	156	4.70	5.00 •	161		4.90	4.85		23.374%	7.36K	-0.1300
RUT	FEB 20 '14 1080 Put	124	5.60	6.00	174		5.70	5.80		22.298%	7.26K	-0.1527
RUT	FEB 20 '14 1090 Put	86 •	6.80	7.20 •	139 •		6.90	7.00		21.498%	4.17K	-0.1830
RUT	FEB 20 '14 1100 Put	114	8.30	8.70	86 •		8.40	8.50		20.732%	3.92K	-0.2195
RUT	FEB 20 '14 1170 Call	317 •	9.50	10.30	151		10.20	9.90		15.411%	3.15K	0.3291
RUT	FEB 20 '14 1180 Call	325 •	6.10	7.00 •	158		7.20	6.55		15.008%	3.44K	0.2536
RUT	FEB 20 '14 1190 Call	255	3.80	4.40	139		4.60	4.10		14.416%	2.29K	0.1823
RUT	FEB 20 '14 1200 Call	122 •	2.25	2.50 •	62 •		2.50	2.38		13.748%	3.44K	0.1199
RUT	FEB 20 '14 1210 Call	97	1.20	1.50	117		1.45	1.35		13.494%	7.36K	0.0773
RUT	FEB 20 '14 1220 Call	95 •	0.60	0.80 •	147 •		0.70	0.70		12.945%	8.20K	0.0429

Figure 8.1

RUT Feb 1020 put

Looking at the choices indicated in figure 8.1, the farthest OTM put that we can sell is the RUT Feb 20 '14 1020 put, and its delta is -.06.

NOTE: If we were to choose to sell the 1010 put, then we would be forced to buy an option not shown in order to complete the spread. Of course, we can do that by adding additional put options to the list of possible options to sell. Here is the problem: You must draw the cutoff line somewhere, or else there would be far too many options and option spreads to examine. In this example, I chose that cutoff when the delta was less than five. You can select a different range of options when making your own trade decisions.

Put description RUT Feb 20 '14 put: This is a put option on RUT, the Russell 2000 Index. The last day that it trades is Thursday, Feb 20, 2014. The following morning (commonly referred to as expiration Friday), the **settlement** price is determined. The strike price is 1020.

NOTE: AT one time all index options were settled at the Friday morning opening. More recently, some index options now expire when the market closes Friday afternoon. Do not trade any index options until you know when it expires. Details can be found at the CBOE, or ask your broker. I am not listing the rules for fear that they may change again.

When the put delta is -6, the chances that the option will be in the money when the settlement price of this option is determined (Friday morning, Feb 21, 2014) are approximately 6%. That is true when market conditions remain essentially as they are when that screenshot was taken. If market volatility declines during that time, the chances become even smaller that RUT will be below 1020 at expiration. If market volatility explodes then it becomes much more likely that the option will finish in the money. In other words, in a more volatile environment, OTM options come with a higher delta (because they finish in the money more often).

NOTE: I have been very careful with the wording in the above paragraph. There is a subtlety that option traders must understand:

--The delta refers to the probability that the option will be in the money *when expiration arrives*. That is 6% in this example.

--That is a very different number from the probability that the option will be in the money at least once between the current time and expiration. The latter probability is referred to as the *probability of touching*. "Touching" occurs when the underlying asset touches the strike price of either short option during the lifetime of the options.

> --Calculators that measure the probability of touching are available. Ask your broker, or try this one:
> (http://www.hoadley.net/options/barrierprobs.aspx?)

--To clarify, delta is NOT telling us the chances that the option will *remain* OTM from the current time through expiration. It only describes the likelihood that an option will be in the money when the option expires.

NOTE: When using any of the Greeks, the numbers are good approximations, but are not meant to be exact. Therefore it is impractical to use more than one or two significant figures. I use only the first two decimal places and in this example, delta is -6.

NOTE: There is no standard agreement as to whether delta ranges from -1.00 to +1.00; or from -100 to +100, and you may choose either scale. I prefer eliminating the decimal and refer to the delta of our example put as being -6, rather than -0.06.

The important points about the delta scale:

> --A put whose delta is -100 is expected to move one full point when the underlying asset moves one point.

> --A call whose delta is +100 is expected to move one full point when the underlying asset moves one point.

> --At-the-money options have a delta near 50.

--Options have a zero delta when they are so far out of the money that a one-point change in the underlying does not affect the value of the option.

The put purchase

There is no purpose to be served by analyzing each of the puts when searching for an appropriate option to buy. Once we carefully select which option to sell (the possibility that the underlying asset will trade at or through the strike price of that option represents the true danger point for the position and is the price that we do not want to see the underlying asset approach, let alone penetrate), it is far easier to choose which option to buy. *Our preference for a specific spread width is so important, that no other factor is worth considering.*

For the following discussion, assume that the spread width (distance between the two call options or the two put options) is 10-points. A more detailed discussion on choosing an appropriate spread width appears in Chapter 14.

If you sell the RUT Feb 20 '14 1020 put, then buying a put that is 10-points farther OTM (RUT Feb 20 '14 1010 put) completes the spread: You would be selling the RUT Feb 20 '14 1010/1020 put spread.

Figure 8.2 repeated for convenience.

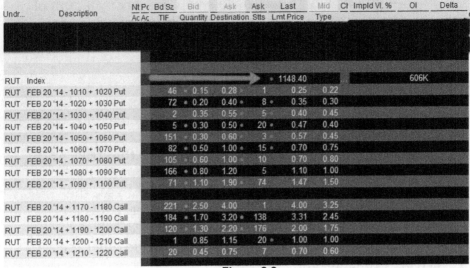

Undr...	Description	Nt Pc Ac Ac	Bd Sz TIF	Bid Quantity	Ask Destination	Ask Stts	Last Lmt Price	Mid Type	Ct Impld Vl. %	OI	Delta
RUT	Index						1148.40			606K	
RUT	FEB 20 '14 - 1010 + 1020 Put	46	0.15	0.28	1		0.25	0.22			
RUT	FEB 20 '14 - 1020 + 1030 Put	72	0.20	0.40	8		0.35	0.30			
RUT	FEB 20 '14 - 1030 + 1040 Put	2	0.35	0.55	5		0.40	0.45			
RUT	FEB 20 '14 - 1040 + 1050 Put	5	0.30	0.50	20		0.47	0.40			
RUT	FEB 20 '14 - 1050 + 1060 Put	151	0.30	0.60	3		0.57	0.45			
RUT	FEB 20 '14 - 1060 + 1070 Put	82	0.50	1.00	15		0.70	0.75			
RUT	FEB 20 '14 - 1070 + 1080 Put	105	0.60	1.00	10		0.70	0.80			
RUT	FEB 20 '14 - 1080 + 1090 Put	166	0.80	1.20	5		1.10	1.00			
RUT	FEB 20 '14 - 1090 + 1100 Put	71	1.10	1.90	74		1.47	1.50			
RUT	FEB 20 '14 + 1170 - 1180 Call	221	2.50	4.00	1		4.00	3.25			
RUT	FEB 20 '14 + 1180 - 1190 Call	184	1.70	3.20	138		3.31	2.45			
RUT	FEB 20 '14 + 1190 - 1200 Call	120	1.30	2.20	176		2.00	1.75			
RUT	FEB 20 '14 + 1200 - 1210 Call	1	0.85	1.15	20		1.00	1.00			
RUT	FEB 20 '14 + 1210 - 1220 Call	20	0.45	0.75	7		0.70	0.60			

Figure 8.2

What do we know about this spread?

--I refer to this as a *"6 delta put spread"* because that is the delta of the option sold.

--The market for this spread (figure 8.2) is $0.15 to $0.28.

--The wide market is $0.15 to $0.45. We get these numbers by combining the bid/ask quotes for the individual options from (figure 8.1):

--Feb 1020 put: $1.80 to $1.95.

--Feb 1010 put: $2.10 to $2.25.

--Best market quote is $0.15 to $0.45; making the midpoint $0.30.

--Notice that someone is offering to sell this spread at $0.28, or two pennies less than the midpoint of the wide market. That spread seller is far more likely to be a retail trader than one of the market makers because it is below the midpoint—and market makers do not advertise when they may be willing to sell something at a reduced price.

--At this point, we have not looked at any other spreads for comparison (we do that below), but I estimate the premium that you can collect for this spread to be $0.25. However, the only way to know for sure is to enter an order and see what happens. You cannot afford to make frivolous trades 'just to see what happens,' so the order is entered only after you decide that this is a trade that you want to make.

For my personal comfort zone, this premium (25-cents) is too small. However, if you are an *inexperienced trader* and want to own an iron condor with a small reward potential and a very good chance of being profitable, this put spread represents a possible trade. Before we can proceed with entering an order, we must do two things:

--Find an appropriate call spread with which to pair the put spread (Chapter 11).

-- Continue checking other put spreads until satisfied that you found one well-suited to your needs.

Back to choosing the put to sell

RUT Feb 1030 put
Delta: -7.

The put spread: Feb 1020/1030 put.

Spread quote: $0.20 to $0.40.

Wide spread quote: $0.20 to $0.50; True midpoint: $0.35.

Estimated premium available: $0.30

Comment: Very similar to 1010/1020 put spread. Premium is $0.05 higher and the option is 10 points less far OTM. With RUT trading at $1148, this spread is 118 points (or 10%) OTM. That is pretty far OTM with 29 trading days remaining.

That option feels as if it is 'safely' out of the money, and the position is well within my comfort zone. But please do not believe that this option cannot become an ITM option. The -7 delta tells us to expect it to be ITM at expiration about one time in 14.

However, the potential reward is 30 cents and this spread is suitable for traders who are willing to accept low profit potential in exchange for a high probability of success.

I often mention 'a high probability of success' for a trade, so let's take a moment to look at the numbers.

The put delta is -7. Assuming we find an appropriate 7-delta call spread, the iron condor position has two short options, each with a 7% probability of being in the money (ITM) when expiration arrives. The probability that *either* option will be ITM (at expiration) is 14% and for traders who hold all the way to that expiration date, the chance of seeing this spread expire worthless is 86%.

The main problem with expecting to earn the entire premium as your profit 86% of the time is that this percentage ignores the times when the spread becomes uncomfortable to hold and must be exited (or adjusted) at a loss—before expiration arrives.

For aggressive, risk-taking investors, that can be when strike price of either the short call or short put becomes an at-the-money option. More conservative traders will have quit the trade well before the underlying asset moves that far.

If RUT were to decline as low as 1030 during the lifetime of the options, then the spread would be worth about $5, or roughly 50% of its maximum value. Sure, the call spread would be virtually worthless at this point, but when we are short a put spread that costs roughly $500 to cover (exit), the fact that the call spread can be covered at a very low price is not much of a consolation. [Strong advice: Do cover that call spread when you exit the put spread. Do not take the risk of a market reversal when the potential gain is so small.] When this happens, the iron condor position is significantly underwater (losing money).

We have not talked a lot about risk management yet (see Chapter 17), but very few traders would consider (correctly, in my opinion) holding an iron condor when one short option is at- or almost at the money. This is not a risk they are willing to take. In fact, most traders would have given up on this trade before the underlying index fell to this level.

The point of this discussion is that the 86% number does not tell the whole story because for some of those 86 out of 100 trades, you (and I) would almost certainly have covered the position and taken a loss, rather than still be holding until the options expire. Reminder worth repeating: The fact that either of the options will be ITM about 14% of the time at expiration ignores the possibility of the option moving into the money (forcing us to exit with a loss) and then moving OTM by expiration.

The conclusion is that even when the options are safely OTM at expiration, you will have been forced to exit (with a good-sized loss) some of those 14 out of 100 trades.

The obvious conclusion is that this 14% number may be statistically accurate, but when managing positions, you cannot ignore risk and blindly count on winning 86% of the time.

Traders require additional accuracy concerning probability. Fortunately such numbers are available by using a "probability of touching" calculator that measures the probability that the underlying asset will move to any specific price *at any time* prior to expiration.

NOTE: You can use any price for the underlying asset; not necessarily the strike price. This can be useful if you want to know the chances that the stock will reach a given price level (if current assumptions —primarily volatility —remain unchanged) by a specific date.

For the newer trader, this is a topic (probability of touching) of lesser importance right now. However it is something worth understanding and a more detailed discussion is presented in Appendix A.

RUT Feb 1040 put

Delta: -8.

The put spread: Feb 1020/1030 put.

Spread quote: $0.35 to $0.55.

Wide spread quote: $0.25 to $0.55; True midpoint: $0.40.

Estimated premium available: $0.35 (available right now because that is the bid, or possibly the true midpoint, $0.40).

Comment: Once again, this is similar to previous choices. Premium is another $0.05 higher and the option is another 10 points closer to the underlying market price (1148). This spread is 108 points OTM.

The remaining puts and put spreads

It may seem tedious to look at every put option (and every call option once you are finished with the puts) to find two spreads that, when combined into an iron condor, are best suited to your personal needs. And if you are a new to trading iron condors (or credit spreads in general), then it is well worth your time to go through a thought process as described above. You do not yet have enough experience to know which options are good alternatives for your situation.

It is tedious. However, this is not a big problem because as time passes (it may only require one or two iron condor trades) and you manage the trades, you should be able discover where your comfort zone lies and therefore cut the initial list of option spreads to a modest quantity. I will offer some ideas on how to get started with something that is likely to be quite suitable for you right now. Then, as you practice (in a paper-trading account) managing iron condors by opening a variety of positions and managing each one from entry to exit, you will discover that you are suddenly comfortable enough to begin trading with real money.

NOTE: It is not important to choose the 'best possible' iron condor because there is no such thing. Instead there are several 'very good' choices that vary from one trader to another.

When using index options (i.e., SPX, RUT, NDX) there are many possible iron condors from which to choose. You will find more than one that feels right (i.e., good for your trading style). That is good. Do not be afraid to trade because you are unable to decide which is slightly better than the other. A large part of the decision comes with knowing what is comfortable to own because only the individual trader knows what it feels like to have a specific position in his/her portfolio.

When trading iron condors on individual stocks, the relatively low price of the stock means that there are not as many strike prices from which to choose. Usually one iron condor choice will stand out, but it is possible that you will not be comfortable with any. When that happens, do not force the trade.

NOTE: It is acceptable to trade a 1-lot iron condor as a learning experience. However, as a long-term strategy, it is important to own positions that make you comfortable. Perhaps this point has not been made sufficiently clear:

When you do not like the idea of owning a position at any point in time, my sincere advice is to fix the position (see risk management, Chapter 17) or exit. The problem with fixing (adjusting) or exiting is that either is likely to reduce profit potential or lock in a loss. As mentioned, having the discipline to take losses is a vital part of the trading game — but traders do not like to take losses. Thus, it is best to avoid uncomfortable positions because you are less likely to hold onto them long enough for the position to produce a profit.

The 10-point put spreads

Table 10.1
The 10-Point Put Spreads

Strike	Delta	Spread	B/A	Wide B/A	Mid
1020	-6	1010/1020	0.15 / 0.28	0.15 / 0.45	$0.30
1030	-7	1020/1030	0.20 / 0.40	0.20 / 0.50	$0.35
1040	-8	1030/1040	0.35 / 0.55	0.25 / 0.55	$0.40
1050	-9	1040/1050	0.30 / 0.50	0.30 / 0.65	$0.48
1060	-11	1050/1060	0.30 / 0.60	0.50 / 0.90	$0.70
1070	-13	1060/1070	0.50 / 1.00	0.50 / 1.00	$0.75
1080	-15	1070/1080	0.60 / 1.00	0.60 / 1.30	$0.95
1090	-18	1080/1090	0.80 / 1.20	0/80 / 1.60	$1.20

Strike = Strike price of option sold
Delta is rounded to nearest whole number
Spread = Strike prices of the two puts that comprise the spread
B/A = Bid and ask quote for *the spread*
Wide B/A = Combined quotes for the individual options in the spread
Mid = Midpoint for Wide B/A quote

The Choice

I would love to provide a formula that you can use to make your selection. The truth is that it is a very personal compromise decision.

--By selling puts that are a little closer to the stock price, the premium (profit potential) increases, but the odds of having a trade that requires no adjustments is reduced.

--By extending the expiration date (see Chapter 15), you can collect a higher premium for the put (or call) spread. Or you can elect to earn the same premium by selling options that are farther out of the money. That may add to your comfort. On the negative side, your capital is tied up in the trade for a longer time AND the longer that you hold the position, the greater the chance that something unfortunate will happen to the index price. Again, it is a compromise.

You must begin somewhere

When a trader goes through the process of deciding wh.
of the several possible put and call spreads to sell, it ma
seem very difficult to come to a decision. The truth is that it
should be difficult because some of the spreads have very
similar risk and reward scenarios.

Thus, I offer the following guidance for newer traders.
Although it is important to make sound choices, please
believe me when I tell you that it the decision becomes less
difficult as you gain experience managing the trades. You
will figure out which positions are safely within your
comfort zone.

If you do not know where to begin, try this:

--Options that expire in two months (8 or 9 weeks).
Alternative: 6 or 7 weeks.

--Spreads that are 10-points wide.

--Selling options whose delta is 7 or 8. However, if you
believe that you are a more aggressive (and less
conservative) trader—and if you are comfortable doing
so— you can begin with delta a high as 9 or 10.

--When you follow the suggestions above, the premium
that you can collect is very dependent on the current
implied volatility. Therefore it is difficult to recommend
a minimum acceptable premium. But, do not accept
anything that you believe is too small to justify the risk.

--Trade size: This is the most important decision of all.
Do not lose more than you can afford to lose. The worst-
case scenario (large loss) will happen, so be prepared. It
is a sound idea to target earning less money while
gaining an options education because your primary goal
is survival. Once you learn how profits and losses arise,
you can adjust your trade size (gently).

Chapter 11

The Call Spread

There are always fewer calls to consider as part of your iron condor than puts. That is a result of the skewed manner that describes how options are priced. In other words, as the options move farther OTM, the premium available from selling call spreads declines rapidly and quickly moves below your minimum acceptable premium.

Figure 8.1 repeated for convenience

Undr...	Description	Nt Pc Bd Sz	Bid	Ask	Ask	Last	Mid	Cl	Impld Vl. %	OI	Delta
		Ac Ac TIF			Stts	Lmt Price					
Feb 20, 2104 PUTS											
RUT	Index					1148.35				606K	
RUT	FEB 20 '14 1010 Put	53 1.80	1.95 •	86	1.45	1.88			28.595%	3.35K	-0.0472
RUT	FEB 20 '14 1020 Put	51 2.10	2.25	135	2.10	2.18			27.691%	5.62K	-0.0554
RUT	FEB 20 '14 1030 Put	55 • 2.45	2.60	112	2.00	2.53			26.769%	6.62K	-0.0650
RUT	FEB 20 '14 1040 Put	58 2.85	3.00	83	2.85	2.92			25.806%	6.33K	-0.0763
RUT	FEB 20 '14 1050 Put	180 3.30	3.50 •	32	3.40	3.40			24.983%	7.85K	-0.0909
RUT	FEB 20 '14 1060 Put	18 4.00	4.20	84	4.00	4.10			24.046%	9.98K	-0.1075
RUT	FEB 20 '14 1070 Put	156 4.70	5.00 •	161	4.90	4.85			23.374%	7.36K	-0.1300
RUT	FEB 20 '14 1080 Put	124 5.60	6.00	174	5.70	5.80			22.298%	7.26K	-0.1527
RUT	FEB 20 '14 1090 Put	86 • 6.80	7.20 •	139 •	6.90	7.00			21.498%	4.17K	-0.1830
RUT	FEB 20 '14 1100 Put	114 8.30	8.70	86 •	8.40	8.50			20.732%	3.92K	-0.2195
RUT	FEB 20 '14 1170 Call	317 9.50	10.30	151	10.20	9.90			15.411%	3.15K	0.3291
RUT	FEB 20 '14 1180 Call	325 • 6.10	7.00 •	158	7.20	6.55			15.008%	3.44K	0.2536
RUT	FEB 20 '14 1190 Call	255 • 3.80	4.40	139 •	4.60	4.10			14.416%	2.29K	0.1823
RUT	FEB 20 '14 1200 Call	122 • 2.25	2.50 •	62 •	2.50	2.38			13.748%	3.44K	0.1199
RUT	FEB 20 '14 1210 Call	97 1.20	1.50 •	117	1.45	1.35			13.494%	7.36K	0.0773
RUT	FEB 20 '14 1220 Call	95 • 0.60	0.80 •	147 •	0.70	0.70			12.945%	8.20K	0.0429

Figure 8.1

Figure 8.2 repeated for convenience

Undr...	Description	Nt Pc Ac Ac	Bd Sz TIF	Bid Quantity	Ask Destination	Ask Stts	Last Lmt Price	Mid Type	Cl	Impld Vl. %	OI	Delta
RUT	Index						1148.40				606K	
RUT	FEB 20 '14 - 1010 + 1020 Put	46	0.15	0.28	1		0.25	0.22				
RUT	FEB 20 '14 - 1020 + 1030 Put	72	0.20	0.40	8		0.35	0.30				
RUT	FEB 20 '14 - 1030 + 1040 Put	2	0.35	0.55	5		0.40	0.45				
RUT	FEB 20 '14 - 1040 + 1050 Put	5	0.30	0.50	20		0.47	0.40				
RUT	FEB 20 '14 - 1050 + 1060 Put	151	0.30	0.60	3		0.57	0.45				
RUT	FEB 20 '14 - 1060 + 1070 Put	82	0.50	1.00	15		0.70	0.75				
RUT	FEB 20 '14 - 1070 + 1080 Put	105	0.60	1.00	10		0.70	0.80				
RUT	FEB 20 '14 - 1080 + 1090 Put	166	0.80	1.20	5		1.10	1.00				
RUT	FEB 20 '14 - 1090 + 1100 Put	71	1.10	1.90	74		1.47	1.50				
RUT	FEB 20 '14 + 1170 - 1180 Call	221	2.50	4.00	1		4.00	3.25				
RUT	FEB 20 '14 + 1180 - 1190 Call	184	1.70	3.20	138		3.31	2.45				
RUT	FEB 20 '14 + 1190 - 1200 Call	120	1.30	2.20	176		2.00	1.75				
RUT	FEB 20 '14 + 1200 - 1210 Call	1	0.85	1.15	20		1.00	1.00				
RUT	FEB 20 '14 + 1210 - 1220 Call	20	0.45	0.75	7		0.70	0.60				

Figure 8.2

For example (see Figure 8.2 or Tables 10.1 and 11.1)), when we consider the RUT 1210/1220 call spread (60-points OTM), the premium is $0.60. Even that premium may be too small for many iron condor traders.

On the other hand, the 60-point OTM put spread (RUT 1080/1090) carries a higher premium ($1.00). More importantly, put spreads that are even farther out of the money can be sold for a higher premium than the 60-point OTM call spread. In this example, the 80-point OTM put spread generates $0.75 while the 60-point OTM call spread offers a smaller premium.

The point of mentioning this characteristic of how options are priced is to be sure that you recognize that this difference exists. Most iron condor traders select positions based on delta (either the iron condor is constructed to be near delta neutral or it is constructed so that the delta of the options sold are nearly equal). I recommend either of those choices. However, if you prefer to trade options that are equally far OTM, then this skewed pricing may produce iron condors that don't feel comfortable to trade.

Table 11.1
The 10-Point Call Spreads

Strike	Delta	Spread	B/A	Wide B/A	Mid
1170	33	1170/1180	2.50/4.00	2.50/4.20	$3.25
1180	25	1180/1190	1.70/3.20	1.70/3.20	$2.45
1190	18	1190/1200	1.30/2.20	1.30/2.15	$1.72
1200	12	1200/1210	0.85/1.15	0.75/1.30	$1.00
1210	8	1210/1220	0.45 / 0.75	0.40/0.90	$0.60

Strike = Strike price of option sold
Delta is rounded to nearest whole number
Spread = Strike prices of the two puts that comprise the spread
B/A = Bid and ask quote for *the spread*
Wide B/A = Combined quotes for the individual options in the spread
Mid = Midpoint for Wide B/A quote

There are two ways to proceed when you have no market bias to consider.

(1) You can go with the put spread that has already been chosen and all you have to do with the calls is find one with a comparable delta.

(2) Let's assume that you chose the 6-delta put spread (1010/1020). From figure 8.1, you can choose to sell the 1220 call (delta 4) or the 1210 call (delta 8). However, you can make the spread nearer to delta neutral by choosing the 8-delta call spread and choosing a different (i.e., 8-delta) put spread. The 1030/1040 put spread fits the bill. [**NOTE**: It is okay to choose put and call spreads with a slightly different delta, but it is NOT okay to choose a different spread width (see Chapter 14), unless the quantity is adjusted.]

If you decide to go with the 8-delta spreads, your iron condor of choice would be:

RUT Feb 20 '14 1030/1040P//1210/1220C iron condor

The cash credit would be approximately $0.90 to $0.95 (midpoint is $1.00).

Before entering the order, take another look at the final choice. There are questions to answer and some of the background information that offers guidance in making the decisions has not yet been covered. It is presented in later chapters). Are you satisfied with the available credit? Even though the spread is delta neutral, are you comfortable being short options with the specific strike prices chosen? Did you choose a reasonable quantity of iron condors to trade? Is the expiration date too far away or too near for comfort? Are you sure that you know how your broker's trade entry system works and that you are NOT buying the options you want to sell? If anything doesn't feel right, take your time to come to a final decision: Trade or don't trade. When ready, pull the trigger.

Chapter 12

Choosing the Underlying Asset

When buying equities, everyone understands that a trader must choose the specific stock he wants to own (or sell short). The trader who works with the whole market or a specific segment, can trade a diversified basket of stocks, such as an ETF (exchange-traded fund), mutual fund, or index fund.

The same principle applies when trading options. However, there is one major difference when trading iron condors: You are not looking for an investment. You are not seeking a stock that will double within a year or two. In fact it is quite the opposite: You want an underlying asset whose price will hold relatively steady over the lifetime of your option position.

> **NOTE:** Do not plan on constructing an iron condor on a dead-in-the-water, very non-volatile stock because the premium on those options is tiny.

Because I cannot offer guidance on how you should pick the stocks that are right for you to trade, I'll offer one suggestion. *Unless you have a reason to trade a specific stock*, the iron condor strategy works best with broad-based indexes. The single most important reason why that is true is that a large collection of stocks is not subject to a wild price swing based on unexpected company-specific news. Because iron condor traders lose money when the underlying undergoes a large price change, it is less risky to own an iron condor position on an index or ETF when compared with an iron condor on a single stock.

It is better (but not mandatory) to trade options that others are trading—options with a significant trading volume where the markets are liquid. For that reason, I recommend the following broad-based indexes/ETFs for iron condor traders:

--SPX (index) or SPY (ETF) that tracks the S&P 500 Index.

--RUT (index) or IWM (ETF) that tracks the Russell 2000 Index.

--NDX (index) or QQQ (ETF) that tracks the NASDAQ 100 Index.

If you prefer to trade a more narrow index perhaps — one with stocks in a single industry, or mid-cap stocks, please have some reason for believing that sector will trade in a narrow range and not be more volatile than the rest of the market.

Chapter 13

Choosing Strike Prices

By now I hope that you appreciate that some compromise is necessary when selecting strike prices for the options that comprise your iron condor position.

There are several considerations in play simultaneously, and the best trade for you has to satisfy all of the following. The trader:

--Wants to own the position. It is not supposed to be a borderline decision. It is better to pass over a trade rather than accept something that you believe is mediocre. There will be plenty of other opportunities.

--Knows in advance

--The maximum attainable profit.

--The target profit when planning to exit prior to expiration.

--The maximum theoretical loss per 1-lot iron condor. This is the most important decision because it helps determine position size..

--The maximum acceptable loss when managing the trade. This should be significantly less than "the maximum theoretical loss."

--Is comfortable accepting the risk in an attempt to earn the target profit.

--Is comfortable knowing that a significant market rally or decline is likely to result in a loss.

To satisfy each of these conditions, you must make a decision regarding the following: expiration date, delta of the options to be sold, spread width, the cash value that it collected upfront, and whether to be delta neutral or to enter the trade with a small market bias.

Because there are several factors to you consider, it is impossible to tell you where you will be most comfortable. However, the idea of choosing an appropriate option is described in detail throughout the book, and you should be able to find a suitable iron condor trade at any time that you believe it is the correct strategy to adopt.

For my trading, I prefer to begin with equal delta (for the options sold) and construct the iron condor from that. That may not be the best choice for everyone. **Warning:** Market conditions change and an appropriate delta today may be inappropriate in the future. It may seem trite, but the best way to know whether the iron condor that you decide to trade is appropriate is to examine your gut feeling. If the thought of owning this position makes you uncomfortable, then it is a poor choice.

Chapter 14

Choosing the Spread Width

At first glance it seems to make little difference which specific spread is chosen, as long as you are very careful when selecting the specific options to sell. However, it makes a large difference.

For example, when deciding to build the iron condor by selling the RUT Feb 1020 put, you could buy the RUT Feb 1010 put, thereby selling the RUT Feb 1010/1020 put spread.

However, if a trader does not recognize the risk involved, it is easy to decide to sell a spread that is 20-points wide (1000/1020P spread), or even 30-points wide (990/1020P spread).

I recommend that you begin by choosing 10-point spreads when your underlying asset is one of the broad based indexes. More on this below.

IMPORTANT NOTE: When trading an individual stock, especially low-priced stocks, 10-point spreads are not likely to be feasible. You should be more comfortable choosing 5-point spreads, 2 1/2 –point spreads, or 1-point spreads, when such choices are available.

> **NOTE:** When trading ETFs, such as SPY, it is crucial NOT to trade 10-point spreads. Those are far too wide. Please understand that a 1-point SPY spread is very similar to a 10-point SPX trade because the asset price is 1/10 as large ($190 vs. $1,900). Thus, 1-point is the recommended spread width for SPY, IWM, QQQ and similar exchange traded funds.

However, 10-point spreads are not for everyone. There can be very good reasons for selling wider call and put spreads, or even the narrower 5-point spreads. For example, if you sell the RUT Feb 1010/1030 put spread:

--The premium collected is larger (almost double).

-- The potential profit is larger.

--THE MONEY AT RISK IS TWICE AS LARGE

IMPORTANT NOTE: It is essential to recognize that money at risk doubles when trading 20-point spreads instead of 10-point spreads. Thus, it is *mandatory* to trade only one-half as many iron condors when the spread width doubles. Similarly, trade only one-third as many spreads when the width triples.

Do not fall into the trap of believing that risk has not really doubled because the underlying has to decline further before you can lose the maximum theoretical amount. Proper risk management requires that you avoid being exposed to a loss that is too large to handle comfortably.

One reason that traders prefer the 20-point spread is to save money on commissions. This seems to be an obvious thing to do. Instead of trading 6-lots of a10-point iron condors, the trader enters an order to trade only 3-lots of a 20-point spread. Risk and reward for the 3-lot and the 6-lot trades are similar. However, commissions are reduced. That seems to be a good thing. However, please be aware of a trap that I want you to avoid. The following discussion is presented at the beginner level to be certain that every reader understands the subtleties.

Two 10-point iron condors vs. one 20-point iron condor

Compare two positions:

Position A:

Sell 2 RUT Feb 20 '14 1090 puts
Buy 2 RUT Feb 20 '14 1080 puts
Credit: $110 per spread; $220 total credit

Maximum possible profit: $220
Maximum possible loss: $1,780 ($890 per iron condor)

Position B:

Sell 1 RUT Feb 20 '14 1090 put
Buy 1 RUT Feb 20 '14 1070 put
Credit: $205

Maximum possible profit: $205
Maximum possible loss: $1,795

The numbers are similar, but not exactly the same. Let's see why this is true.

Equivalent position

Let's consider buying two different 10-point spreads. This is merely an example, and you would never enter the following two orders:

Sell 1 RUT Feb 20 '14 1090 put
Buy 1 RUT Feb 20 '14 1080 put

Sell 1 RUT Feb 20 '14 1080 put
Buy 1 RUT Feb 20 '14 1070 put

When you theoretically make both trades, the 1080s cancel and you are left with a position that is short the 20-point, 1070/1090 put spread. This is universally true when the two 10-point spreads have one strike in common.

NOTE: If you prefer to trade the 20-point spread, do it in one transaction. Enter an order for the wider spread and never trade both spreads because it would be a significant waste of money. [Extra commissions plus buying and selling the option with the common strike price (1080, in this example) costs money in slippage.]

Choosing spread width

Here is the lesson in a nutshell. When considering which 10-point spread to trade, it is very often true that you will find a single spread that most closely fits your objectives for the trade. When that is true, it makes sense to make that trade. In the above example, when you compare the 1080/1090 and the 1070/1080 put spreads, you will discover some obvious differences:

--The 1080/1090 put spread is closer to the money and you can collect a slightly higher premium.

--The 1070/1080 spread is farther out of the money and there is a slightly smaller chance that RUT will decline far enough to cause problems.

--The 1090 put has a -18 delta and the 1080/1090 put spread is expected to be (at least partially) ITM at expiration about 18% of the time. The 1080P has a -15 delta and the 1070/1080P spread will be in the money (at expiration) about 15% of the time.

--Note that these differences are real enough that most traders can reach a decision and choose between them.

Trading RULE: Choose the narrower spread when possible, as long as you truly prefer that specific position. If you like both equally, then that is the time to trade the wider spread—and that gives you the same position as trading an equal number of each of the more narrow spreads. If you have a real preference, do not trade the wider spread just to save a few dollars on commissions. Instead trade the spread that you prefer to own.

There is a totally different school of thought for traders who want to be short strangles (short put and short call). I cannot recommend this strategy to anyone, but it should only be adopted by very experienced traders who are willing to take the risk of being naked short options.

They believe that buying options to complete the iron condor is a waste of money. They may choose the iron condor trade for the sole purpose of reducing margin requirements. This group is not concerned with risk (a poor decision) and tends to trade very wide (50- or even 100-point) spreads because they have to buy *something* to get that margin reduction, and they want to spend as little cash as possible. This is something that I discourage.

I hope you appreciate the importance of spread width. It is not merely an afterthought. It is an important part of the decision-making process because it establishes your maximum possible loss for the trade. The primary consideration remains choosing which put (and call) to sell, but choosing the proper spread width is not to be ignored.

Chapter 15

Choosing the Expiration

Expiration Style

Options are either American style or European style and the description has nothing to do with where the options are traded.

American style options may be exercised by their owners at any time before the options expire. Upon exercise, 100 shares of the underlying stock are 'traded.'

--Call owners buy stock from call sellers.

--Put owners sell stock to put sellers.

--All transactions occur at the strike price.

--**Note** for inexperienced traders: If you buy (cover) an option sold earlier, you no longer have to be concerned with the exercise/assignment process.

European style options may be exercised only at expiration. Thus, there is no such thing as 'early exercise' of this option type.

These options are cash settled. When expiration arrives, all owners of an in-the-money option receive, in cash, the intrinsic value of the option. The cash is transferred from the accounts of traders who sold (and did not cover) those options. At-the-money and out-of-the-money options expire worthless. This is very convenient because no shares change hands.

The major index options (except for OEX) are European style and that is another reason why they are appropriate options for iron condor traders. [Early exercise could become a serious risk issue if you unexpectedly had to buy via assignment) an ITM option – because you would have had no chance to balance your position before the market opens.]

Expiration date
When it comes to picking the expiration date, much depends on the individual trader. Long-term iron condors are inappropriate for the vast majority of traders and I recommend not using options with expiration longer than four months, unless there is some special situation.

Very short-term (weekly) iron condors
The indexes that I recommended for iron condor trading—along with ~300 of the more actively-traded stocks—have listed options that expire every week. These options are very much of a good news/bad news story. Time decay is rapid and when trading these very short-term iron condors, you will love the rate at which you can make money.

On the other hand, these options cannot be very far out of the money at the time they are sold (because time is so short that they would be essentially worthless), and that means any decent-sized rally or decline quickly places these spreads at risk of losing money.

It is the Greek 'gamma' that allows us to measure this risk. [Reminder; gamma is the rate at which an options delta changes when the underlying moves one point. It is those rapidly changing deltas that make an option appear to have limited value one minute and considerable value the next.]

The bottom line is that these weekly iron condors are for traders who want more action. That means higher reward for greater risk.

My opinion: These are not for newer traders. Get some iron condor risk management experience before tackling these. Wait until after some of your trades have gone awry and require that you make a decision regarding risk. When you open a position and exit with no problems, that does not count towards risk-management experience.

For traders who prefer to work with short-term options, I find it is better to trade these options with a directional bias. Thus, I use the single credit spread, rather than the iron condor when I want to be bullish or bearish for a few days. When truly market neutral, I prefer iron condors with lifetimes that range from one to three months.

Moderately short-term (30-day) iron condors

Unless you want to trade very-short term options, these are the most often selected expiration dates for traditional iron condor traders.

The major tradeoff is as it is with all iron condors:

> --The fewer the number of days before expiration, the faster the time decay,

> --More time allows you to sell farther OTM options and still collect a good premium.

My opinion: Begin with a 2-month iron condor and see how you feel about the trade as it progresses. Newer traders should sell options with a delta of 7 to 8 while experienced traders can choose something appropriate for themselves based on that experience.

If you are impatient with the 2-month position (after giving it a trial), try a shorter expiration time frame for your next trade. If you like being short options that are farther out of the money and if that makes you feel comfortable, you may want to try a 3-month expiration for your next trade.

> --For the conservative trader, my favorite iron condor involves index options that expire in 12- or 13-weeks. The options sold have a delta of ~15 and the spread width is 10-points. I require a premium near $3.00 ($2.75 to $3.30). In today's (mid-2014) market environment, implied volatility is very low (VIX = 11) and it is impossible to generate such high premium.

> --3-month options are rich in vega (another of the Greeks that measures the sensitivity of an option's premium to a change in the implied volatility (IV)). For

it reason, it makes sense to sell 3-month options only
...en IV is already above average. Why? Because if you
are short vega (and all iron condors are short vega) as
implied volatility increases, the spreads that you sold
will increase in value. The market may not move much
and your position may look quite safe, but the higher IV
means that money has been lost and you would have to
hold for a longer time than originally anticipated to earn
the desired profit. The longer the position is held, the
more time there is for something to go wrong. Thus:

Bottom line: Do not sell 3-month (or longer-term) iron
condors unless IV is high enough to provide a $3
premium on the 3-month, 15-delta iron condor.*

*Definition: A 15-delta iron condor is one in which the
options that you sell each have an approximate delta of
15. The spread width does not affect the definition.

   --If market conditions are not right for a 3-month iron
   condor, then I suggest durations of 6 to 8 weeks for
   conservative traders.

   --The one-month iron condor was (by far) the most
   popular iron condor before weekly expiration dates
   became available. It is still a good compromise
   position for those who want more rapid time decay
   but who do not want the added risk that comes with
   the extra negative gamma associated with weekly
   options.

Long-term iron condors
I do not recommend iron condors with lifetimes longer than
4-months. LEAPS options do exist and you can collect a
nice premium for a 2-year LEAPS iron condor. However,
time decay is very slow and who knows where the market
will be in one year, let alone two? Iron condor traders earn
money from time decay and there is little reason to tie up
your cash to meet margin requirements) for such a long
time.

Chapter 16

Deciding when to Exit

Traders face three decisions every day for each position in their portfolios:

--Do nothing and hold.

--Adjust or modify the position. (More on this in Chapter 17.) One possible modification is to close a portion of the position, or using the language of traders, reduce position size.

--Exit.

By far, the most common decision is to hold and await developments. In other words, once you own an iron condor position, most days you will discover that the position is safely within your comfort zone and that there is no reason to take any action.

However, it is important to recognize that deciding to hold is as much of a decision as any other. It is easy to get into the (bad) habit of holding the trade for 'just one more day' to see what happens. I encourage you to take time each day:

> *Examine each position.*
>
> *Decide: Do you like this position well enough to hold?*
>
> *Has the position become too risky?*
>
> *Would it be beneficial to adjust or exit?*
>
> *Should you consider an exit because the position earned its target profit?*

Much of the time, it will be obvious that you want to hold. But getting into the habit of examining what you own can only improve your results. Complacency is the enemy of a profitable trader.

Because the iron condor earns money as time passes (and nothing unpleasant happens to the stock or index price), holding is a painless decision and an easy one to make.

However, there will be times when holding doesn't feel right. I must caution you not to hold positions for the sole reason that you do not know what to do. A true novice has a good excuse for not knowing which specific risk-management action to take, and may be hesitant to act. That is one good rationale for using a paper-trading account to gain risk-management experience. The more experienced trader should be able to make a sound "hold or adjust" decision. When you are not confident about such a decision, then my advice is to compromise by closing part of the position to reduce size.

NOTE: That does not mean buying back your short options. That is not closing "part of the position". However, it does mean buying back one- or more lots of the call or put spread that is in trouble. If your trade consists of only one-lot, then this choice is unavailable.

Sometimes by looking at the risk graph provided by your broker you may discover all the clues needed to make a good decision. When you see how much money can be lost if certain events happen (the stock price moves 1, 2, or 3%, or if some days pass, or if IV increases), you will know whether such events will leave you in good shape or whether defensive action is necessary. For example, if your loss is small (by your standards) when the stock price changes by 2% today, then you should not panic when the price does change by that 2%.

What you want to do is take another look at the risk graph and determine the stock price at which you would no longer be comfortable owning the position. **By the way:** If you do this risk graph study at the time the trade is initiated, you can devise a trade plan that covers several "what if" scenarios. When you have a trade plan, it becomes much easier to manage the trade on a day-to-day basis because some "adjust now" decisions have already been made.

If you find yourself in the position of not really knowing whether your comfort zone boundaries have been breached, you are probably best off holding for another day (or hour or however often you can re-examine the position). Why? Because newer traders tend to panic by adjusting too soon and it is less common for them to panic by refusing to take action.

Keep in mind that any trader can (and should) be afraid of potential losses, and that is the reason for writing a trade plan. By making decisions in advance, you will not have to make such decisions in the heat of battle. For example, when the maximum acceptable loss has occurred, then it is exit time. It is not the time to think about alternatives.

The experienced trader can make a more detailed decision. He/she should have some experience with adjustment methods and that makes it much easier to decide whether one of those methods (Chapter 19) is appropriate at this time.

But the basic advice still applies. If you do not want to hold the position, do not own it. If you are truly undecided as to what action to take, exiting one-half the position becomes a decent compromise.

Exit; Covering the position

You can adopt one of three basic plans when exiting:

--Exit only when expiration arrives and allow the chips to fall where they may. (This is a bad strategy.)

--Exit any time that you are satisfied with the profit.

--Exit at any time that the position becomes too uncomfortable to hold.

As an intelligent trader, you must be flexible and allow your judgment to play an important role in all decisions. Yet, the three basic choices above cover the gamut of possibilities. Let's examine each, looking for flaws.

1. Hold to expiration

In my opinion this is the worst possible choice. Yet it is fairly common among unsophisticated traders. It is acceptable to decide to hold to the end for any given trade (for the right reasons), but it should not be a basic part of your general strategy.

The argument goes something like this: When the trade was made, you knew the maximum possible loss, and that loss must have been acceptable (even if undesirable). If it was acceptable then, it should be acceptable now. Hold the position and let luck play a big role in your results.

If you believe that you have some skill when trading (why are you willing to risk money if you do not believe you have such skill?) or are currently learning the necessary skills, then do not allow luck to play such a large role in your results. Only traders who lack such skill or who don't understand what they are doing should depend on luck. Just know that doing so is gambling, not investing and certainly not trading.

Luck always plays a big part in our trading profits. Trading iron condors is a statistical game—and we know the probability of success/failure. When we make an 80% play we expect to win 80% of the time. However, we cannot allow any of those losses, which occur 20% of the time, to wipe out the profits from the winning trades. For that reason, it pays to manage the position and not to hold all the way to expiration. In other words, when we are in one of those losing trades, we can cut losses and do not have to risk taking the maximum theoretical loss on the trade.

Clarification: The maximum acceptable loss (this is far less than the maximum theoretical loss) that you wrote into your trade plan is just that: a maximum. Sound risk management techniques should prevent your losses from reaching that point too often.

Looking back on your trades, if your profit/loss ratio is close to 100%, then recognize that you had a bit of good luck. If your ratio is near 50%, then things did not go your way often enough.

You cannot change good or bad luck, but you can make good decisions that move the odds of achieving a winning trade further in your favor. When your profit/loss ratio is exceptionally high or low, it is important to study the results and determine the role that luck played in your results. If you never adjust and always hold to expiration, then your results are going to be based on luck. If you are not making sound risk-management decisions, then you cannot expect to find success.

If you must hold; if you must seek the maximum possible profit; then please recognize that profits can disappear quickly when expiration nears. Using the language of traders, keep your position size small.

Remember this: Once you are earning money from any position, that profit represents your money. Do not take extra risk with that money thinking that it belongs to "the house".

2. Exit when happy
What can one say against this philosophy? If you get out of the position any time that

--You achieved the profit stated in the trade plan.

--You have so little possible profit remaining that it does not pay to risk an adverse market move to earn that small sum.

Example

You trade an iron condor with a 6-week lifetime, collecting a $200 premium. After 4-weeks you can exit by paying $0.30. That would represent a profit of $1.70 or 85% of the maximum. To most traders, that is good enough when you consider than anything can happen in the remaining two weeks. You still like the position, but a prudent trader may decide that enough is enough.

--The underlying index has been rising steadily, but enough time has passed that you currently have a small profit (or a small loss). You are thrilled not to be losing money considering the price of the underlying index. Rather than tempting fate, you decide to get out while you are still pleased with the results.

3. Exit when uncomfortable

--Traders who can pull the trigger on this decision are those who will become successful. You have so many opportunities to make new trades that it makes no sense to own any position that makes you uncomfortable.

--You changed your mind and currently believe that the market is very likely to be more volatile in the very near future. You may not be 'happy' with the current profit/loss picture, but this is a position that should be closed or adjusted.

--The position is far from neutral because the underlying index has undergone a decent-sized price change. If the market continues in that direction for another day, your loss (as estimated by using risk charts and the Greeks) will be more than you can tolerate. This position is too risky and you should not want to own it any longer. It may be tempting to hold for just one more (one more day, hour, minute, or ??), but do not fall into that trap. This is where good discipline proves valuable.

--You earned nearly all the available profit and are afraid that it could disappear. This decision may be motivated by fear, but that is acceptable for traders with a bit of experience. The novice is likely to be fearful of too many different situations and that is why small position size is essential (it helps reduce fear).

--Do allow fear of taking a big loss help you get out of positions with too little remaining reward potential. A common example of this occurs when expiration week arrives and the iron condor can be covered by paying $0.05 for the call spread and $0.05 for the put spread. Each spread may seem to be safely out of the money, but for a small sum, all risk (and fear) can be eliminated. This is an ideal time to exit, if you haven't done so earlier.

--Almost anything can cause a trader to be overly concerned with a specific position. Perhaps a major news announcement is due in one or two days and you fear how the market will react. There is nothing wrong with exiting now, just for the peace of mind that it brings.

It is always acceptable to close your position and exit. It is not always the decision that leads to the best result because an adjustment may improve the risk/reward characteristics of the potion, but it is always a reasonable choice. In addition, you must understand how risk-reducing trades work before applying them.

That's next.

Part III

Managing Risk

Chapter 17

Basic Risk Management

There are two basic ways to invest:

--Invest your cash and hold forever.

--Constantly reevaluate your holding and make changes when necessary.

I am not Warren Buffett, whose preferred holding period is forever. Nor can I discover the outstanding investment opportunities for the future. I recommend that investors periodically examine every investment and decide whether it still belongs in your portfolio. If yes, and if the price has appreciated so that this holding is larger than the average holding, sell a portion to balance the portfolio. Next, use the cash for another investment, or re-allocate the funds to something other than equities.

Very long-term investors can work on their holdings once or twice every year, and that should suffice. If you write covered calls, then checking the status of each position every couple of weeks probably serves your purpose.

But iron condor traders are not for investors. They are used strictly as a shorter-term trading strategy. As such, I encourage you to examine each position every day. Why? Because at some point in time, it is very likely that you will no longer want to hold the position as it currently exists. That happens:

--When the position reaches its target profit.

--When the remaining gain is too small to be worth any risk.

--When IV surges or when the underlying asset price changes, money has been lost. The probability of losing an additional sum has increased to an unacceptable level.

Real vs. 'Paper' Loss

Let's assume that you make a trade and collect (for example) $200 per iron condor. A few days pass and the market rallies by 3%. If you want to get out of the position, it would cost $250 per iron condor.

Most people like to think of this as 'only a paper loss.' If they continue to hold they "know" that they have a good chance to recover that loss and eventually earn a profit on the trade.

It is true that they have a good chance to recover and profit. However, the loss is real (but unrealized). What is not true is that 'it is *only* a paper loss.' This is not the place for a discussion about the philosophy of trading, but I want you to understand that this is a real monetary loss.

When you look at this position, you have two choices.

--Exit and accept the $50 loss.

--Hold and await developments.

There is nothing wrong with holding and, in fact, although we are not looking at the specifics of this trade, it is very likely that almost every trader would elect to hold because this position is not very different from the starting position (delta of short options is not much higher).

However, the one reason for holding that is unacceptable is: refusing to take a loss. If I do hold, it must be because:

--I like the position at its current $250 price and would prefer to hold rather than exit.

--I am comfortable with the position. That means:

--The delta of the short options is not too high for my comfort zone.

--The number of points (or percentage of the underlying asset price) that my short options are out of the money is not a concern.

--Imminent risk has not increased beyond my comfort level. (More on this below).

--The dollars lost is less than the limit mentioned in my trade plan.

Imminent Risk

When you make a trade for which a change in the underlying price results in a loss — and the iron condor is such a position — then you should have an idea of how much further the underlying price can change *today* before you become nervous about further losses. In other words, if short RUT 1150 calls, your trade plan should include a price at which you would seriously consider taking defensive action. That price point depends on many factors and I cannot offer specific guidance that suits every reader. However, by using risk graphs, you should be able to figure out a price level (or a delta level for the 1150 calls) that makes you uncomfortable.

Example

If you would never hold a short option position when its delta is 25 or greater, then this information has to be part of the trade plan. It would be foolish to initiate the trade by selling calls and puts whose deltas were 20 at the time of the trade. That '20-delta' number is just too close to your discomfort point of 25-delta. It would make far more sense to begin with a delta closer to 10.

If you would never be comfortable holding a short RUT call spread when the short option is less than 30-points out of the money, then the original iron condor should not be only 40- or 50-points out of the money. You must own a position where (statistically speaking) an adjustment will not be required most of the time. To profit, time must pass. That means that there is an opportunity for the underlying price to change – and you cannot afford to own a position where the odds are high that your comfort zone will be breached.

The point of this discussion is to offer one more idea for the thinking trader. It may seem trivial, yet it is seldom discussed. Let's call it a very strong suggestion, rather than a rule:

> *Do not initiate an iron condor position when it is highly likely that it will move outside your comfort zone before your planned profitable exit.*
>
> *This minimizes the need for making adjustments.*

Gamma

As time passes and as expiration nears, two things change for the iron condor position: Profits accumulate when the underlying asset behaves; and negative gamma increases. The reason you are concerned with that negative gamma is that the option delta can change very quickly when gamma is high and a "safely-out-of-the-money option" can quickly move into the money. That results in a significant loss (the loss is more severe when little time remains before expiration arrives).

The different iron condor types

Earlier, I mentioned four different types of iron condor— and the fact that each should be managed differently. Below is a very brief discussion:

1. Far OTM iron condors generate little premium, but the probability of earning a profit is high. The difficulty with owning this position type is knowing when to cut losses and exit. For example, looking at a 10-point iron condor for which the premium was $0.25, no one would want to suffer the maximum loss of $9.75, but discovering a comfortable time to exit is difficult.

If you are the type of person who exits early and often – to insure that nothing terrible happens — then you will have too many losing trades. If this FOTM IC strategy does not result in a winning trade at least 90% of the time, then (from my perspective) your overall profits will be too small and this strategy will not be viable. If you earn the full $0.25 nine times in 10, then the one loss must be less than $2.25 for you to break even – let alone earn a profit. If you take that loss when the price reaches $1.00, then you may be exiting more often than one time per 10 trades. It is truly a management quandary.

If you never adjust, refusing to take any loss, every once in a while the position can lose enough money to cancel 2- or 3-years' worth of profits (assuming one trade every month). That is not viable either.

This strategy presents a true dilemma and I urge you not to trade cheap iron condors. I cannot tell you what represents a minimum premium for your trading style. If you are new to the iron-condor game, then I suggest a reasonable place to start is not accepting less than $0.55 for a 1-week iron condor or $1.00 for a 4-week position.

2. Trading CTM (close to the money) iron condors requires a very different mindset. First, the options sold have a higher delta than your standard iron condor (that is part of the definition of a CTM position), and the options may be close enough to being ATM that the trader wants to make an adjustment because the position is uncomfortable to own.

If that is how you feel, then do not trade this iron condor type. It makes no sense to own positions that are uncomfortable to hold. However, if you understand the rationale for owning CTM positions, then it should be very comfortable to see why there is nothing scary about trading CTM condors.

Rationale for this (CTM) IC type:

--The premium is high (perhaps $3.50 to $4.50 for a 10-point iron condor). Therefore, the maximum possible loss is less for this trade than for other iron condor trades. Although you will have fewer trades that work perfectly — i.e., you get to cover at your desired profit level with zero adjustments — but those few trades produce very high profits.

--If the underlying asset undergoes a price change and one of the short option is at the money, or almost at the money (delta between 40 and 50), it becomes time to adjust the position to reduce risk. The recommended adjustment is the roll down. Translation: cover the ATM spread and sell an equal quantity of another spread of the same type (i.e., if you covered a call spread, sell a new call spread; if you covered a put spread, sell another put spread), such that the spread sold expires at the same time and is farther out of the money. The cost depends on implied volatility and costs less when IV is high.

--The roll down will cost $200 to $300, depending on how you choose the strike price of the new spread, implied volatility, and the number of days that remain before the options expire. However, the cost to roll is almost always going to be significantly less than the original premium collected. In other words, you own a new iron condor and your remaining cash premium is no longer high, but is high enough for you to be able to come out of the trade with a decent profit – as long as another adjustment is not necessary. And that is pretty much standard operating procedure for iron condor traders: One adjustment leaves room for a profitable trade, but most of the time that a 2nd adjustment is necessary, the profit (if any) will be small and a loss is likely.

--Once the position has been rolled down, the iron condor is not going to be very different from the traditional iron condor (described in the next bullet point), The option spreads will be far enough out of the money that you have a decent chance to earn a profit.

--This is the mindset that has to be understood for you to be comfortable trading CTM iron condors: Think of this newly adjusted position as being quite similar to one that you might have chosen for your original iron condor position. True, the residual premium will be a bit less than you could have collected for this position earlier, but in return, you had a chance (if no adjustment had been needed) to exit with a very good profit. So, if you have a position similar to a more traditional iron condor and if the premium is not hugely different, then holding the CTM iron condor caused no harm and you were able to handle the risk management decisions appropriately.

--One other benefit of trading CTM iron condors. Because the premium is high, you can afford to trade smaller size and have even less money at risk per trade.

3. Very short-term (one- or two-week) iron condors. There is a reason why options that expire weekly have become very popular among individual investors. For option buyers, the premium is lower and a big, quick stock price change can provide large profits. For option sellers, time decay is very rapid and profits can be earned quickly.

Warning: These are tricky to trade and require the talents of an experienced iron condor trader. In the previous sentence, the term "experienced" refers to someone who has successfully handled decisions involving when and how to adjust positions. It does not refer to a trader who has opened and closed several iron condors without having to face difficult risk-management decisions.

The obvious rationale for owning a one-week iron condor is that you can earn a very nice profit in ~3 days (I encourage exiting no later than Thursday afternoon when the options settle at Friday's opening prices). The problem is that the premium is small and the iron condor options are not very far out of the money.

Deciding whether to hold another day to collect the time decay comes with taking the risk of a rapidly-increasing loss when the stock price is moving. This is a difficult situation for inexperienced risk managers. It is easier to gain useful experience by trading the traditional iron condor (below).

4. Traditional iron condors. It is impossible to define a "best" iron condor to trade because the first requirement is that the position must be comfortable to own — and each of us has a different idea as to what is comfortable.

Thus, by my definition, the traditional iron condor is the position you prefer to trade when you DO NOT want to own "something different." In other words, you would not be choosing an iron condor that fits into one of the three previous categories.

A few years ago when IV was higher, my traditional iron condor was a 13-week, 13- to 15-delta, 10-point RUT iron condor with a premium of $3.00 ± $0.30. In today's low IV world, it is impossible to achieve a premium anywhere near that level. Thus, do not expect to select a favorite iron condor type and trade it forever. Market conditions change and you must accept that fact. In more recent times, I chose to trade shorter-term (one to four-week expirations), rather than trade 13-week positions with a reduced premium. Experiment and find something suitable for your needs. Being comfortable is important. Please do not force a trade when you do not truly want to make that specific trade.

The most important aspect of risk management is to recognize when it is necessary to change the risk characteristics of your position. It is not a good idea to initiate a position and let the chips fall where they may. The idea behind proper risk management is to take your profits when then are available and to minimize—when appropriate— the possibility of suffering a large loss.

Chapter 18

Advanced Risk Management: The Concept

If you decide to make an adjustment (other than reducing size or exiting) to an existing position, then there are numerous possible adjustments. In the next chapter we will examine a few specific examples. But first, more discussion is necessary.

An adjustment trade serves one purpose: It reduces risk.

--Sometimes the probability of losing money (from the adjustment point into the future) is lowered.

--At other times the adjustment is a reduction in the total cash at risk (i.e., the maximum possible loss).

> **An adjustment is not a desperate attempt to take a trade that has lost money and magically turn it into a profitable trade.**

The philosophy of adjusting positions

An adjustment should not be made just because you refuse to accept the fact that the current position has lost money.

It is far more intelligent to unload (exit) a bad position and buy a new position, one that you believe has a much better chance to earn a profit – from the time that the position was adjusted into the future -- and not counting from the time that the original trade was made.

It is important to understand why adjustments are made. This may seem trivial, but too many traders 'adjust' risky positions with the hope that all will turn out well in the end. That is not trading. That is not adjusting. That is gambling.

> **The adjustment is made to protect the assets in your account and generate future earnings. It is not made to recover past losses.**

What is an adjustment?

An adjustment for any option position consists of any trade that accomplishes EACH of these objectives:

1. Imminent risk is reduced. In other words, if the price of the underlying asset continues to move in its current direction by a specific amount, you will lose significantly less money after making the adjustment compared with the unadjusted position. **NOTE:** It is not necessary to remove all risk every time an adjustment is made. The objective is to convert the position into one that is comfortable to hold.

--To meet this objective, reduce delta exposure. In other words, when the position is short delta, add some positive delta to the position. When long delta, add some negative delta to the position.

--Add positive delta by *buying* calls or call spreads. Add negative delta by *buying* puts or put spreads. I urge you not to sell additional put or call spreads to pick up the needed delta – because that increases ultimate risk. If you insist on selling, rather than buying spreads, please cover the current short call (or put) portion of the iron condor before selling more call (or put) spreads.

--That 'specific amount' depends on your comfort zone and how rapidly money will be lost if you do not adjust.

--I suggest two alternatives for deciding how much that specific move should be:

--**Percentage**. Perhaps 1, 2 or 3%. Look at a risk graph to see how much money would be lost on a rally/decline. Choose a percentage such that the potential loss is well within your acceptable limit.

106

You always want to take defensive action before any loss is large enough to make you uncomfortable (i.e., angry with yourself for not taking steps to reduce risk earlier).

--**Standard deviation** (SD). One or 1.5 standard deviations

--Where: One SD = S * V*SQRT (t/252)

--Where: S = stock price; V = volatility estimate as a decimal between 0 and 1.0; t = number of days, and 252= # of trading days in one year. It is acceptable to use 365 days instead, but the result will be very different.

--For this calculation, t = 1 because this is a one-day standard deviation calculation. The idea is to decide how much the stock can change price today before you must take action. Obviously you can use a one- or two-week calculation to make future risk-management plans.

Example

RUT is 1200.00 and V = 0.15

SD = 1200 * .15 * $\sqrt{(1/252)}$ = 1200 * .15 * 0.063 = 11.34

Look at the potential profit/loss when RUT moves approximately 11 points. If the loss is within, but approaching the border of your comfort zone, then make an adjustment when RUT moves 11 points today.

Important clarification: Do not make the serious mistake of ignoring each day's price change when it does not result in an adjustment trade.

--If RUT is 1200 when you plan the adjustment and if you decide to adjust after a one day's 1.0 standard deviation price change, then you want to adjust when RUT hits 1211 (or 1189).

--If RUT rallies to 1204 today, 1206 tomorrow , 1210 the next day, and 1215 one day later—a 15-point move that may leave you believing that none of those price changes was large enough to trigger an adjustment on its own. That is an inappropriate conclusion. However do not automatically adjust:

If your decision is to consider adjusting every time that RUT moves one (or some other quantity) standard deviation, then once RUT hits 1211 (or 1189) take another look at the risk graph. Do not make an automatic adjustment. Determine whether that adjustment is still needed. **NOTE**: It may not be needed because the passage of time often makes the position much less risky to own at 1211 now, than it would have been a few days ago. Calculate a new adjustment point and ignore the previous calculation.

--This may seem complicated, but all you are doing is deciding every day where to adjust *today*, if something unwanted happens to the price of your underlying asset. There is nothing special about 1.0, 1.5, or any other number of standard deviation moves. Traders use these numbers as a reminder to pay attention to the price changes, encouraging them to take a fresh look at the current risk profile – after such a move occurs.

2. The newly adjusted position must still satisfy the premise of owning any option position.

--You are pleased to have the position in your portfolio.

--The probability of earning a profit (from this point in time into the future) is good.

--The possible profit is good enough to justify current risk.

--Most important of all is being sure that you did not make this adjustment for the sole purpose of avoiding the unhappiness that comes with locking in a loss. It is far better to take the loss and open a brand-new position that meets all of your investment criteria.

3. **The position being adjusted is worthy of salvage**. Some positions can become unwieldy (i.e., after an adjustment or two, it may contain too many different options) to manage. Other positions may be too stressful to manage simply because you spend too much time worrying about what to do next. Don't be concerned with these position types. Unload them and find new trades. Reducing risk is the primary objective when adjusting, but reducing stress is another worthwhile goal.

4. <u>**Prime Directive**</u>:

> **The trade that you make as an adjustment MUST earn money as a standalone trade whenever the original (currently threatened) trade continues to lose money. Never create a position such that it is possible for the adjustment to lose money at the same time that the pre-adjustment position continues to bleed money. NEVER.**

The adjustment does NOT have to earn more than the original trade loses. It just has to offset PART of that loss. If you prefer to offset the entire loss, then it is better to simply exit the trade. Adjustments are hedging trades that are intended to reduce losses, not eliminate them.

This is the whole idea behind adjusting. The adjustment must earn a profit to offset at least a portion of any additional loss that accrues to the original position.

It is not good enough when the risk graph looks good. The adjustment trade (if it were a standalone trade) must never lose money when the original trade is losing money. That is the reason why buying farther OTM options is unsuitable. The passage of time and a small market move (in the wrong direction) would increase the loss.

It is not good enough to examine what happens at expiration. Nor is it good enough to calculate what happens the day that the adjustment is made. The adjustment trade must earn some profit when the original trade loses money.

Chapter 19

Advanced Risk Management: Examples

There are always a bunch of alternative strategies that you can use when adjusting an iron condor position. Remember that the adjusted position must be less risky to own than the pre-adjustment position.

When it comes to adjusting iron condors, please recall the suggestion that iron condors should be *managed* as if they were two separate positions. In the text below, when I refer to the "threatened" side or the "at risk" portion of an iron condor, that reference is to *either* the call spread as the market rallies, or the put spread after the market declines.

There is one overriding rule for adjustments:

> ***Do not add risk. Do not increase position size.***
>
> ***Be certain that the newly adjusted position cannot result in a larger loss.***

Exception: If you are under-invested, it is acceptable to increase position size.

For example, if you usually own 10-lots of three different, 10-point, iron condors simultaneously, then your normal allocation is 30 10-point iron condors. If you have only two such positions and one of them requires an adjustment, it is acceptable to bring your total (for all positions) up to 30-lots. In other words, you may—if the trade is very appealing—adjust the threatened iron condor so that it becomes a 15- or 20-lot position. I'll discuss how this works in one of the examples below.

DO NOT abuse this exception because it is far too easy to blow up a trading account by continuing to sell extra spreads. Sure it feels good to bring in extra cash, but you know that it is not sane to expect every option to expire worthless. Why would you want to allow for the possibility of taking a bit hit when an unexpected rally or market debacle occurs?

Important NOTE: The ideas below are presented with sufficient detail that you can adopt any of them with confidence (when you are certain that you understand the purpose behind making the adjustment trade). There are no shortcuts in the descriptions. However, the serious trader may discover that he/she still has questions. A topic such as managing iron condors includes so many details that it requires a lengthy book of its own.

Strategy 1. Cover

Cover positions that are very "cheap." If either the call spread or the put spread reaches a very low value (difficult to define, but it can be $0.05 to $0.20, depending on how much time remains and the premium that you collected when opening the position), buy it. There is too little residual potential profit for you to take the risk of remaining short that spread.

If for example, the market is falling and the put spread is getting into trouble and you are thinking about making a risk-reducing adjustment, it probably makes sense to pay $0.10 to $0.20 cents to cover the call spread. The primary rationale is to avoid risk when there is almost nothing to be gained. Holding onto this position because it is so far out of the money is not a good idea when it costs so little to cover.

When the market has moved far enough in either direction that money has been lost, and the losing portion of the iron condor requires an adjustment, do not be afraid to spend a small amount of cash to cover the other portion of the original iron condor. It is easy to tell yourself that you already lost money on this trade and you refuse to add to the overall loss by spending any money on the cheap spread. Do not believe that it is worth the risk associated with waiting for the options to expire worthless.

Strategy 2.The Replacement Spread.
If you do cover a short spread as described above, there is a prudent adjustment method available. It is not something that has to be done, so be sure to decide whether this is appropriate for this specific set of conditions.

The *sole purpose* behind this adjustment is to turn your current position into one that is closer to market neutral. It will not be delta neutral, but this adjustment is closer to market neutral than the pre-adjustment position. This method is not suitable for every trader, so if you do decide to adopt this idea, please be very careful to follow *all* suggestions below.

Of all the strategies mentioned in this chapter, this one produces the least amount of risk reduction. It is still acceptable under the right conditions and you should understand how it works. However, it does not reduce negative gamma and the "at risk" portion of the iron condor remains just as risky as it was.

--Sell another spread (obviously, if you just covered the call spread, that means sell another call spread).

--DO NOT anticipate. In other words, do not sell the new spread unless the spread being replaced has already been bought. The disciplined trader may sell the new spread first, but ONLY when he/she immediately purchases the spread being covered. Bidding is not good enough. If you are not sure you can cover at a price that you are willing to pay, then be conservative and cover first and sell the replacement spread second.

--The new spread should have the same expiration date as the covered spread.

--The new spread must leave you comfortable with the new risk. This is important: If you just covered the call (or put) spread, then you have zero upside (or downside) risk. Thus, selling this new spread reintroduces upside (downside) risk.

--The premium must meet some minimum standard. You do not want to introduce upside (or downside if the trade involves puts) risk for a small reward.

> **VITAL MINDSET: Never think of this trade as a way to cut losses if the market continues to move in its current direction. The premium available by rolling a call or put spread is just too small to act as a meaningful hedge when the market continues its current trend.**
>
> **This trade is made for one reason only: You do not have a market bias and want to convert the position to one that is closer to delta neutral.**

Many times there is nothing suitable to sell and your choice becomes holding or choosing another adjustment strategy.

a. The time remaining before expiration arrives should not be too short because the premium will be too small and the negative gamma will be too high. This "sell a replacement spread" is not feasible when less than two weeks remain in the lifetime of the options. In other words, if you are trading weekly iron condors, this is not a good adjustment strategy.

b. Repeating a crucial message: You must avoid a losing way of thinking. Make this trade only when you want to bring the position closer to neutral. Do not make this trade believing that it is free money (because you think the market will continue to move in its current direction. If you believe that to be true, then get out of the entire iron condor because it is not a suitable strategy when you have a significant bullish or bearish market bias.)

> ***Never sell this replacement spread unless you have already covered the father out-of-the-money cheap spread.***

Strategy # 3a. Buy expensive delta and gamma.

When the market is moving one way and the position is becoming too risky for you to own it as is, then make an adjustment by cutting risk. The most effective way to do that is to reduce both delta and gamma risk. That is accomplished by buying something.

You can buy **individual options**: Buy puts when the market is falling and your position has too many positive deltas; buy calls when the position has too many negative deltas. The problem with this idea is that the calls and puts are expensive and you may be unwilling to spend so much cash to protect a position from danger.

> ***One Warning: Never (that means never) buy options for protection when they are farther out of the money than the option you are currently short.***

EXAMPLE

If you sold the XYZ 1200/1210 call spread, the only call options you can buy for an (intelligent) adjustment have a strike price of 1200 or LOWER.

115

(Yes, it is OK to buy some of the option you are short—the 1200 call).

If you sold the XYZ 1200/1210 put spread, the only put options you can buy for an (intelligent) adjustment have a strike price of 1210 or HIGHER. (Yes, it is OK to buy some of the option you are short—the 1210 put).

When buying those "farther out-of-the-money than your current short" options, the risk graph may look good, but the risk of losing a lot of money increases. So why does the risk graph look so good? Because it shows what happens on a gigantic market move.

Owning extra options always looks good when the market cooperates. However, in the vast majority of cases, the market does not rally/decline by 10 to 20% just because you own a few extra OTM options. The most likely event is that those options will expire worthless.

This is not a big deal when the options are bought for speculation. If you want to take a chance and buy those cheaper, far OTM options, go for it. You will lose almost every time, but may get lucky once or twice. But, when buying options for PROTECTION; when buying options to REDUCE RISK, these options are unsuitable.

The problem with buying protection for very uncommon events (the big move) is that money will be lost on the vast majority of trades. Trades that are intended to reduce risk should reduce risk 100% of the time. They should not contribute to the possibility of additional losses.

If time passes and the market continues its rally (or decline), here is what will happen when your adjustment consisted of buying options that are farther OTM than your short options: The options you bought will still be OTM and will lose value. The spread you are short will (possibly) move ITM and its value will increase. As a result, you not only failed to reduce losses for the at-risk portion of the iron condor, but the adjustment trade results in an additional loss.

That is not acceptable when adjusting a position.

Strategy #3b. Buy much less expensive delta and gamma.

Instead of buying puts or calls, you can buy a small number of put or call spreads.

Buying option spreads: Buy put spreads when the market is falling and your position has too many positive deltas; buy call spreads when the market has been rising and your position has too many negative deltas. The protection is limited, in contrast with buying single options where the protection is unlimited. However, it costs far less to adopt this adjustment strategy, and that is important.

EXAMPLE

If you sold the XYZ 1200/1210 call spread, then you want to buy a position that will make money when this spread is losing money. That is what makes it an adjustment.

As when buying individual options (Strategy 3a), the spread must not be farther OTM than your current short spread. Thus, depending on the cost of each spread and how much protection is needed, consider any of the following (or use your imagination) as suitable adjustments:

--XYZ (same expiration) 1180/1190 call spread.

--XYZ (same expiration) 1185/1195 call spread.

--XYZ (same expiration) 1190/1200 call spread. Yes, it is acceptable to sell more of the option that you sold earlier, as long as you also buy an option that is closer to the money.

--XYZ (same expiration) 1200/1210 call spread. Yes, it is often a good idea to adjust by buying some of the option spreads that you sold earlier.

--XYZ (same expiration) 1180/1185 call spread. The spread width can be a different. This one is narrower.

--XYZ (same expiration) 1175/1190 call spread. The spread width can be different. This one is wider.

Whereas owning an extra call (or put) option or two could be enough to offset all future losses (think gigantic market move), it is intended to reduce future losses. Thus, if you were short 10 of these call spreads, the adjustment may be to buy 2-3 of the new call spread. If the market continues to rally, you may choose to make another adjustment, or you may decide that it is best to give up on a trade that did not work well and exit. If you do exit, once again close the position by using limit orders. Never use market orders.

If you sold the XYZ 1200/1210 put spread and the market is falling, then you must buy a position that earns money when this spread 1200/1210 put spread is losing money.

Thus, the only option spreads you can buy for an adjustment are put spreads with strike prices of 1210 or higher.

EXAMPLE

--XYZ (same expiration) 1225/1215 put spread

--XYZ (same expiration 1220/1210 put spread

--etc.

> **Big warning: Do not pay too much for the spread. If you buy a 10-point call spread, the most it can ever be worth is 10 points, or $1,000. If you pay $800, then you add $800 worth of downside risk and all you gain is $200 worth of upside protection.**
>
> **Suggestion: Limit the purchase price for any spread (that is bought for the purpose of reducing risk) to 40% of its maximum value. That means pay no more than $4 for a 10-point spread, $2 for a 5-point spread, or $0.40 for a 1-point spread.**

Strategy #4. The pre-adjustment

I like the idea of owning a position that comes with a built-in adjustment for those times when you fear a market move, but still want to own an iron condor position.

For example, instead of selling 10 put spreads and 10 call spreads, initiate the trade as if you already made an adjustment:

When SPX is trading at 1950, and you fear a severe market correction, you could make this trade:

Sell 7 (or 8) 1890/1900 put spreads and
Sell 10 1990/2000 call spreads

That sample iron condor assumes that an adjustment has already been made. In other words, the iron condor began life as a 'normal' 10-lot position, but that you bought 2- or 3- lots of the put spread as an adjustment.

NOTE: The short put is 50-points out of the money and the short call is 40-points out of the money. This is a common situation when traders prefer to initiate the trade with a position that is near delta neutral. Traders who prefer "distance neutral" would choose the 2000/2010 call spread instead.

Strategy #5. The Broken-Wing Iron Condor

Another example of a pre-adjusted iron condor is the "broken wing" variety. The trader elects to open a broken-wing position instead of a regular iron condor.

This iron condor variety uses the strategy of skipping one or more strike prices. This is not a market neutral position because risk is greater to either the up- or downside.

EXAMPLE

The put BWIC (Broken-Wing Iron Condor) position comes with greater downside, and reduced upside, risk.

Buy 8 SPX Jul 1880 puts
Sell 8 SPX Jul 1900 puts (the 20-point put spread)
Sell 8 SPX Jul 1990 calls
Buy 8 SPX Jul 2000 calls (the 10-point call spread)

Net cash: $550 per iron condor.
Maximum loss when SPX is above 2000 at expiration:
$450 * 8 = $3,600.
Maximum loss when SPX is below 1880 at expiration:
$1,450 * 8 = $11,600.

NOTE: If you are familiar with the concept of equivalent positions, you know that the 20-point spread is equivalent to two 10-point spreads. Thus the BWIC above is the same as an ordinary iron condor in which 16 (eight each of the 1880/1890 and 1890/1900) 10-point put spreads but only 8 of the 10-point call spreads are sold.

Strategy # 6. The OTM calendar spread

This adjustment strategy is included for the sake of providing a variety of methods. However, the user must be very careful because it is possible to violate the Prime Directive when buying OTM calendar spreads.

The trade: Buy a calendar spread with a strike price that is near the strike price being protected. The calendar spread may be a little less far OTM, or a little further OTM.

EXAMPLE

Your iron condor is short 10 Oct XYZ 950/960 call spreads.

The adjustment: Buy 2-4 of any ONE of these calendar spreads:

XYZ Nov/Oct 945 call spread
XYZ Nov/Oct 950 call spread
XYZ Nov/Oct 955 call spread

Calendar spreads gain value when:

1. The underlying asset moves from its current price and approaches the calendar spread strike price.

2. Additional profit is earned when time passes and #1 is true.

3. Conclusion: As the price of XYZ moves toward the strike price of one of the short options, the iron condor is usually losing money. However, the calendar spread slowly earns money that *partially* offset losses.

Important facts about buying OTM calendar spreads:

--Call spreads are bought to gain upside protection. Put spreads are bought to provide downside protection.

-- Protection is limited. Do not adopt this strategy when you fear a substantial rally or decline. When the underlying continues to move beyond the calendar's strike price, the accumulated profits tend to disappear.

--This strategy is very dependent on the implied volatility of the options. Thus, in general, expect it to provide less protection when protecting the call side of the iron condor (IV declines on most rallies) and to work better when protecting the put side of the iron condor (IV tends to increase on market declines).

-- Calendar spreads begin to lose value once the options move into the money. Translation: DO NOT CONTINUE HOLDING THE CALENDAR SPREAD ONCE THE OPTIONS ARE ITM OR ALMOST ITM because that violates the prime directive. On a further rally (or decline), the iron condor would continue to lose money as the calendar spread begins to lose value.

This trade can be used effectively, but it cannot be used often. The ideal market conditions are quite limited.

Strategy #7. Selling Extra Option Spreads
This strategy has a lot of appeal, especially for traders who fall into one of two categories:

--The less-experienced trader.

--The trader who does not fully grasp the concept of risk.

EXAMPLE

The following iron condor runs into trouble as the underlying stock rallies to $480 (from $440):

Sell 6 XYZ Nov 360/370 put spreads
Sell 6 XYZ Nov 490/500 call spreads

One *reasonable-looking* adjustment is to cover the **six** call spreads and sell **twelve** XYZ Nov 520/530 call spreads. The resulting position is an off-balance, far from neutral iron condor:

Short 6 far-OTM 360/370 put spreads
Short 12 not-so-far-OTM 520/530 call spreads

Why this trade is appealing:

--The adjustment can be made without spending much cash. When implied volatility (IV) is high, the "roll down" trade can be made for a cash credit. In other words, it does not cost any out-of-pocket cash. When IV is much lower, you must pay a small debit to make the trade.

This is attractive to the trader who hates to spend cash on any adjustment. **NOTE:** Spending cash is not a bad thing because the adjustment is made to reduce risk. Its primary purpose is to avoid taking a substantial loss and not to search for a chance to exit (eventually) the trade with a profit. It may "feel safer" to be short spreads that are farther OTM than they were pre-adjustment, but being short twice as many is a losing strategy (Martingale) over the longer-term.

Why this trade is unappealing (i.e., too risky)

--It is not "much safer" to be short twice as many options (or option spreads). True, the probability of losing additional money is far less, but the amount at risk is far more. Do not confuse "a high probability of earning a profit" with "safe." To me, a safe position is one for which the worst-case scenario results in an acceptable, not a portfolio-destroying, loss.

--It exposes you to a loss that is much larger than your original trade plan allows. If you abandon the plan to take on additional risk, that will become a bad, difficult habit to break.

--The trader learns to depend on a doubling-down approach based on the Martingale system. The strategy has the gambler double the bet after every loss, so that the first win recovers all previous losses plus a profit equal to the original stake. Unless you have an infinite sum to invest, the odds are high that you will eventually go broke.

--Although doubling position size from 6 to 12 (in this example) is not a terrible idea in itself, the problem

123

occurs when this trade has to be adjusted two more times and you find that the margin required to carry a 48-lot position is beyond your means. The trader who successfully adopted this strategy one time will be anxious to adopt it again and again – and that begs for trouble.

--The only time that I recommend this strategy occurs when you are underinvested and increasing position size for one specific trade keeps your portfolio within its position-size limit.

The bottom line for adjusting positions is that the iron condor must be adjusted into something worth owning. When position delta and gamma are reduced (i.e., you bought options or spreads), the adjustment will serve its purpose.

The risk-management ideas in this chapter should be more than enough to get you started as a risk manager.

Afterword

The purpose behind preparing this volume is to give readers a very solid understanding of the iron condor and how to make each of the important trade decisions. That includes some ideas on specific trades to manage risk.

It is important to mention that this is not intended to represent a complete course on trading iron condors. My goal is to provide more than enough information for readers to understand how the trade is supposed to work and what can be done when the trade goes awry.

Most importantly, I hope I have introduced you to concepts not found elsewhere in the options-trading literature and that you will use these ideas to your advantage. I believe it is helpful to understand the experienced trader's mindset as trade decisions are being made. When those thoughts make sense, you have a plan to follow – at least when getting started. When those thoughts don't feel quite right, you have an opportunity to make changes. The benefit to every reader is that this education process gets you thinking about the whole strategy. Too often a book and its lessons are taken as gospel and the reader becomes a rote trader, rather than a thinking trader.

There is more to learn about this strategy, and much of that will come from your own trading experiences and perhaps in discussions with other traders.

I encourage you to think for yourself and not to accept everything that you read or encounter on the Internet as The Truth.

Good trading to all.

Appendix A

Probability of Touching

As iron condor traders, you will often want to get a good handle on the likelihood that the short options will expire worthless. The corollary is the probability that an option will expire in the money. NOTE that this probability ignores *the stock price between the present time and that future expiration date.* It is only concerned with the expiration price.

Unless you are a trader who always (and inappropriately, in my opinion) holds positions through expiration, there is a different probability number – one that is far more relevant when trading iron condors. That is the "probability of touching," or the odds that the stock price will reach (i.e., touch) a specific price *at any time* on, or prior to, a future date. This specific price is most often the strike price of the short options in the iron condor, but the calculation can be made for any price using any future date.

For example, you may want to know the chances that the stock will trade at any price within the next week or two (or any other date).

'Probability of Touching' Calculators

Fortunately calculators that generate the necessary numbers are readily available. Your broker may have a 'probability of touching' calculator. If not, I like the one offered by Peter Hoadley . It is free to use, but the free version allows only a few calculations per session. Find it here: http://www.hoadley.net/options/barrierprobs.aspx?

Why is this calculator worth using?

The inexperienced iron condor trader looks at the delta of the short options (assume it is 8) of an iron condor and correctly decide that the chances of that specific (call or put) option being in the money when expiration arrives is 8%.

He may incorrectly conclude that (if held to expiration) this iron condor will expire worthless 92% of the time.

The first problem is that each short option has an 8% chance of being in the money. Thus, if held until the options expire, the position expires worthless only 84% of the time. In other words, one of the options will be ITM for 16% of the trades.

The second, and more important, problem is that markets do rally or decline without waiting for expiration to arrive. Thus, the call or put spread may move into the money before expiration. When that happens, the trader is unlikely to continue to own the position and will very likely exit. The probability that this occurs cannot be ignored. Also consider that the short option does not have to be ITM before the position becomes too uncomfortable for most traders to hold.

Thus, the position may be worthless at expiration 84% of the time, but a good risk manager will never hold that position that often. There are always going to be instances when you elect to get out of the trade just because it has become too risky to hold.

Thus, the 84% (expiring worthless) number is not of practical use. The probability of touching the strike price is far more important because it tells you how often you can anticipate holding until your preferred exit date (expiration or perhaps one or two weeks earlier).

> *The thinking trader can use this calculator to generate even more useful information.*

EXAMPLE (using the Hoadley calculator)

Given: Your iron condor's short options are struck (have strike prices equal to) at 800 and 900. The underlying price is 850. Expiration is 45 days in the future. Volatility is 15.

--The probability that the underlying price will touch *one* of the options before expiration is 53% (see figure A.1 below). The chance of touching *both* strikes is near zero.

--If the underlying were more volatile (25), then the probability of touching would be much higher (92%). See figure A.2. The chance of suffering the indignity of seeing both short options touched is 9%.

--If you plan to exit the trade in three weeks, then change the number of days to 21. If you also plan to exit the trade when either option is only 20-points out of the money, then change the boundaries to 820 and 880. See figure A.3. The calculator says that you would exit 65% of the time. That is too often and this calculation should tell you to avoid this specific trade if you plan to exit at 820 or 880 within the next 21 days.

These calculations provide great information on what to expect over the course of the trade. Obviously these are probability calculators and they cannot be used to predict the future.

Hoadley Probability of Touching Calculator
45-day; 15-Volatility Iron Condor

Figure A.1

Current stock price:	850.00
Upper boundary price:	900.00
Calendar days:	45
Expected return on stock: Help	1.50 % pa
Hours/trading day:	6.5
[Calculate]	

Lower boundary:	800.00
Volatility: (>1%)	15 % pa
Dividend yield:	0.00 % pa
Trading days/year:	252

...bability functions are available in the Finance Add-in for Excel

Probability Analysis

Measure	At period end — At end of day 45	At any time during the period — Assuming continuous monitoring of prices	Prices monitored hourly each trading day	Prices monitored once per trading day	Prices monitored once per week
Probability of price being above upper boundary price	14.09%	28.05%	26.26%	23.66%	19.07%
Probability of price being below lower boundary price	12.31%	24.72%	23.08%	20.70%	16.53%
Probability of price touching either boundary price		52.61%	49.24%	44.31%	35.59%
Probability of price touching neither boundary price		47.39%	50.76%	55.69%	64.41%
Probability of price touching both boundary prices		0.16%	0.10%	0.05%	0.01%
Probability of price being between boundary prices	73.61%	100.00%			

Hoadley Probability of Touching Calculator
45-day; 25-Volatility Iron Condor

Current stock price:	850.00			
Upper boundary price:	900.00	Lower boundary:	800.00	
Calendar days:	45	Volatility: (>1%)	25	% pa
Expected return on stock: Help	1.50	% pa	Dividend yield:	0.00	% pa
Hours/trading day:	6.5	Trading days/year:	252	

Calculate

Probability functions are available in the Finance Add-in for Excel

Probability Analysis	At period end	At any time during the period			
Measure	At end of day 45	Assuming continuous monitoring of prices	Prices monitored hourly each trading day	Prices monitored once per trading day	Prices monitored once per week
Probability of price being above upper boundary price	25.02%	50.73%	48.11%	44.21%	37.08%
Probability of price being below lower boundary price	25.21%	49.75%	47.22%	43.43%	36.49%
Probability of price touching either boundary price		91.79%	88.85%	83.65%	72.19%
Probability of price touching neither boundary price		8.21%	11.15%	16.35%	27.81%
Probability of price touching both boundary prices		8.69%	6.48%	3.99%	1.38%
Probability of price being between boundary prices	49.77%	100.00%			

Figure A.2

Hoadley Probability of Touching Calculator
21-day; 15-Volatility Iron Condor

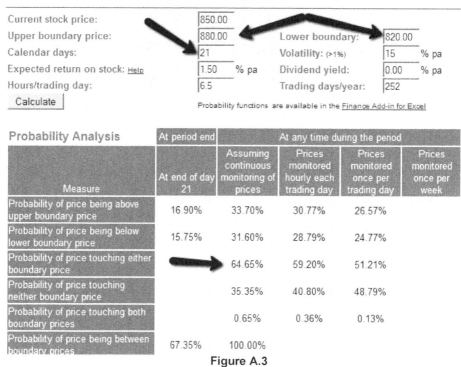

Current stock price:	850.00		
Upper boundary price:	880.00	Lower boundary:	820.00
Calendar days:	21	Volatility: (>1%)	15 % pa
Expected return on stock: Help	1.50 % pa	Dividend yield:	0.00 % pa
Hours/trading day:	6.5	Trading days/year:	252

Calculate

Probability functions are available in the Finance Add-in for Excel

Probability Analysis	At period end	At any time during the period			
Measure	At end of day 21	Assuming continuous monitoring of prices	Prices monitored hourly each trading day	Prices monitored once per trading day	Prices monitored once per week
Probability of price being above upper boundary price	16.90%	33.70%	30.77%	26.57%	
Probability of price being below lower boundary price	15.75%	31.60%	28.79%	24.77%	
Probability of price touching either boundary price		64.65%	59.20%	51.21%	
Probability of price touching neither boundary price		35.35%	40.80%	48.79%	
Probability of price touching both boundary prices		0.65%	0.36%	0.13%	
Probability of price being between boundary prices	67.35%	100.00%			

Figure A.3

Most rookie iron condor traders fail to recognize – because it is not a common situation – that the market may occasionally force them to exit one part of the iron condor and then reverse direction and wreak havoc on the remaining side. The probability of touching calculator can be used to see just how likely that is to occur. It is the "probability of price touching both boundary prices."

To avoid that catastrophe, I urge you to cover the call or put spread at a low price at the same time that you faced the unhappy prospect of taking a loss on the other portion of the iron condor. I understand how painful it can be to spend a little more cash when you just had to cover the other half of the iron condor. But this small sum is money well spent, even if it is just for peace of mind.

Thank you for buying Iron Condors.

Join my e-mail list for occasional updates:
http://blog.mdwoptions.com/sign-email-list/

Visit my blog: http://blog.mdwoptions.com

- For 1,000 great articles about trading options.
- Special promotions and discounts.
- Information on new books.

Other Books by Mark D Wolfinger

My Dead-Tree Books:

The Rookies Guide to Options, 2nd Edition (2013)

Create your own Hedge Fund (2005)

The Short Book on Options (2002)

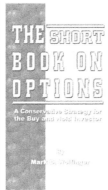

The Best Option Strategies Series of eBooks

Book One. (Volume 0) Intro to Options: The Basics (2014).

Book Two. (Volume 1) Writing Naked Puts (2014).

Book Three (Volume 2) Iron Condors (2014).

My other eBooks:

The Short Book on Options (2002, 2014)

The Option Trader's Mindset: Think like a Winner (2012)

Lessons of a Lifetime: My 33 years as an Option Trader (2010)

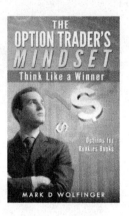

About the Author

Mark Wolfinger has been in the options business since 1977, starting as a market maker on the trading floor of the Chicago Board Options Exchange. He is now an author and educator of individual investors, specializing in the conservative use stock options.

Born in Brooklyn, New York in 1942, he currently resides in Evanston, Illinois with his life partner Penny.

He received a BS degree from Brooklyn College and a PhD from Northwestern University (Chemistry).

His blog: http://blog.mdwoptions.com
He writes on options for about.com: http://options.about.com

Made in the USA
Monee, IL
10 March 2020